THE ONE.

SPIRITUAL TRUTH, MYTH, LEGENDS & FOLKLORE

DOUG McPHILLIPS

Other Visionary Stories

Novels

From Darkness to Light.
The Sword of Discernment.
Santiago Traveller.
I, Prophet.
Awake to my Gutted Dream.
We is Me Upside Down.
The Guru of Jerusalem
Masters at my table.
The Wicklow Way.
The Adventures of Ace McDice,
Stretch Deed & Moonshine Melody.
Instant karma and grace.
Reflections of an Old Man.
The Credo.
King of the O' Malley.

Albums

Country Camino. Album
Santiago Traveller. Album
Soul Fact. Album

Doug McPhillips 2023.

ISBN 978-064-58862-2-1   eBook 978-064-58862-3-8

This book is copyrighted. Apart from any fair dealing for the purpose of private study, research, criticism or reviews permitted under the Copyright Act, no part may be reproduced by any process whatsoever without the editor's permission.
 National Library of Australia Catalog-in-publication data: Holy Bible, New International Version 1980 edition.   HolyBible, Revised Standard 1989 edition: pilgrimage, Mark K. Shriver, Random House, New York, 2 016. Academia letters, Google research, Authors unknown.
 The Mythic Journey.Liz Greene and Julie Sharman Burke- Simone & Schuster 1999.

Content

Introduction. 5.

Chapter 1. The Relevance of Myth. 9.

Chapter 2. The Spiritual Quest. 19.

Chapter 3. Finding the inner Grail. 31.

Chapter 4. The play of unending life. 41.

Chapter 5. The love of the One. 47.

Chapter 6. Testimony of The One. 57.

Chapter 7. In Christ's Reformation. 67.

Chapter 8. Gospel Reflections. 75.

Chapter 9. The Manifested One. 83.

Chapter 10. The Shadow of God. 91.

Chapter 11. Epilogue. 101.

Introduction.

Throughout the ages, primitive tribesmen have wandered the earth for food, clothing and shelter. The earliest of these nomadic tribes whose ancestors still live in this modern age is the Australian Aboriginal. Between 65,000 and 80,000 years ago, a small band of humans landed in Northern Australia. This has been confirmed by over 11,000 artefacts uncovered in archaeological digs in Kakadu National Park. The findings have rewritten the consensus understanding of human occupation in Australia. The ocean crossing from Africa to Asia to Australia is one of humanity's outstanding early achievements but is shrouded in mystery.

It is suggested early humans the Australian continent on rafts made of bamboo, a common material in Asia. With the last Ice Age in progress during the now known, tribes hunted in the north of Australia. Perhaps they walked across frozen ocean islands, breaking the frozen ocean belts and progressing on rafts between ice patches to make it. Whatever the means, judging by modern habits, they studied the stars and were guided by them.

The early Aboriginal nomads undoubtedly told stories of 'The Dreamtime,' passing them to their offspring. Stories of strange Gods and beings in the stars who shaped the continent. These mythical tales have been handed down from generation to generation, changing in the telling, but basic myths remain. Native Aboriginals still go walk-about (nomadic wandering) to hear tribal elders speak of ' The Dreaming,.' the mythical stories that bind the Aboriginals to this continental land. The Australian Aboriginal oral literature consists of stories traditionally performed by Aboriginal people of all groups across Australia. All such myths variously tell significant truths within Aboriginals Aboriginal group's local landscape. They effectively layer the whole of Australia's land topography with cultural nuance and deeper meaning, and they empower selected audiences with Accumulated wisdom and knowledge of their ancestors back through time immemorial.

A mythical map of Australia would show thousands of characters varying in importance, but all connected to the land somehow. Some emerged as specific sites and stayed in that vicinity, others came from somewhere else. Many shape-changing, transformed from or into human beings or nature species, or into natural features such as rocks, but all left something of their spiritual essence at the places noted in their stories.

So many myths are gathered from the images from the sky, and some ancient links to specific star patterns as one might imagine in the readings of the signs of the zodiac in Astrology. Perhaps the most significant of star signs that parallels Christian belief is that of the birth of the one known as the 'Sacrificial Lamb.' Suffice it to say that like so many similar stories in cultures that have evolved through Greek and Roman times to the present day, the stories in this book will bring to life the spiritual essence of those myths and how they relate to humanity today.

The legends of oral stories evolved into written language in ancient Greece. The ancient Greeks didn't invent the alphabet, though they may be credited with inventing an alphabet – a new form of alphabetic writing, one that added signs for vowels to signs for consonants. Their alphabet is the world's first fully phonetic alphabetic script, which emerged sometime around 800 BC. The Hebrew alphabet, which is the groundwork from which the Jew's religious scrolls and related myths came to be, is actually about the same time as the Greeks wrote their stories and original mythical beliefs.

The ancient Romans had a rich mythology, and while much of it was derived from their neighbours and predecessors, the Greeks, it still defined the rich history of the Roman people as they eventually grew into an empire. The history of the Roman Empire lasted from (625 BC to AD 476).

Greek gods are given a beautiful, perfect physical appearance, while Roman gods are not given physical form and are represented only in the people's imagination. Greek gods are mainly based on human personality traits like love, hate, honour and dignity, and myths related to them are shaped by these traits. Roman gods are based on objects or actions rather than personality traits. The actions of gods and mortals in Greek myths are more individualistic; the deeds of an individual are more influential than those of the group. Deities were necessary for the progression of life in Greek mythology, but mortals were just as crucial since their contribution to society mattered in the end. In Roman mythology, the heroic deeds of gods were more important than the actions of mortals, as man's life did not matter once good status in the afterlife had been achieved. In Greek myth, the perspective is more concerned with the physical life on Earth than the afterlife. Mortals are remembered and rewarded for their good deeds on earth. In contradiction, the Romans, in their mythologies, believed that by good deeds, they could secure their place in Heaven. They believed they could earn a place among the gods and strove towards this goal throughout their earthly life. Like the Greeks, Romans had many monuments to the gods, both living and dead. They even had one of worship to "'The God of the unknown." During the latter period of the Roman Empire, a man was born that eclipsed all the myths and foretelling of the Aboriginals, the Greeks and the Romans. The Old Testament of the Bible, its myths and storytelling, speaks of the coming of the chosen one, as recorded from the prophets of old.

Whilst everything we gather as insight is given to us through the content of consciousness, we as ever-evolving humanity gradually crystallise our ' presupposes,' as we have always done in the search for certain knowledge since the first beginnings of philosophical thought. In our modern habits of meditation to escape the madding crowd, we still suffer the chaos of chattering voices in our heads. This as we know from history caused Socrates to make the statement" I know nothing." Descartes found that doubting and therefore thinking leads us to realisation. And of such it is evident that we are more self-aware today, more conscious of being aware of something, be that only the surprise of uncertainty in our philosophy of life and in the facts and the fiction of myth that making of fact gives us something to cling to or overcome the fear of letting go. We do not know if we are deceiving ourselves in our logical forms of thought. We cannot verify beyond certain limitations the content of our consciousness, we cannot ascertain anything as certain beyond our sense of perception and it is uncertain for us to know the substance of anything beyond the phenomena of it all. So in short let me sum up this introduction by saying that myth-making has its place in logic as much as the creative imagination has its place in this storytelling.

This little story that follows unlocks the meaning and the relevance of myth, sacrifice and suffering. It is an introduction to guiding oneself into the ultimate purpose of living in this world but not of it. It led this author to the life on earth of one man who understood all of the legends and myths before and after his allotted time whilst he walked this earthly plain and it uncovers his message of salvation as it applies today. It is a little guide to enlightenment about the chosen spirit I call "The One." Now read on.

CHAPTER 1.

THE RELEVANCE OF MYTH.

The Aboriginal ancestry, the oldest of humanity to this day, used myths and legends to interpret messages from the patterns of the constellations of stars and passed them on to offspring as a kind of wisdom for living in this world, but not of it. The messages were about survival and understanding, the invitation to learn from elders' long-term experience, the lessons of hunting for food to nourish the body, clothing to protect and dress in accordance with climatic conditions, and finding shelter without making any one location a permanent home. More than anything else, they were taught how to be wise by studying the stars. Aboriginal myths and mythology generally describe the journeys of ancestral beings, often giant animals or people, over what began as a featureless domain. Mountains, rivers, waterholes, animals and plant species, and other natural and cultural resources came into being due to events that took place during 'Dreamtime' journeys, and their existence seen by indigenous people confirms their creation beliefs.

Aboriginals believe all their myths across Australia represent a kind of unwritten oral library within Aboriginal peoples, learning about the world and perceiving a peculiarly Aboriginal 'reality' dictated by concepts and values vastly different than those of Western societies. For the Australian Aboriginal, the sky was a textbook of morals and stories retold around campfires. They had their signs of the Zodiac made of fish and dancing men in a backdrop to existence for tens of thousands of years. For example, the bright stars Arcturus and Vega appeared in winter, and the Arnhem land tribes knew it was their sign to lay fish traps. They learnt from the God of fire in the night sky the controlled use of fire to back-burn the land for regrowth in spring, as equally as they used fire for warmth in cave dwellings or roasted and smoked kangaroo or what the earth provided in vegetation and by experimentation what was edible and what was not. Aboriginal myths and mythology generally describe the journeys of ancestral beings, often giant animals or people, over what began as a featureless domain. Mountains, rivers, waterholes, animals and plant species, and other natural and cultural resources came into being due to events during 'Dreamtime' journeys. There they learnt to read the signs in the sky of living on the earthly plane. Accepted and honoured the earth's benefits bestowed upon them by the Gods who, through their education and mythical stories, believe and pass on from generation to generation the facts of their spiritual existences as much as their human needs to survive. From the earliest Aboriginal man, the consciousness of the inherited propensity for infinite enlightenment persisted as vital as the urge of a plant to seek the sun.

Likewise, the Greeks, in their own enlightened age, believed in the myths and legends of their times. At the centre of Greek mythology is the pantheon of gods and goddesses who were said to live on Mount

Olympus is the highest mountain in Greece. From their lofty perch, they ruled every aspect of human life. Olympian deities looked like men and women (though they could change into animals and other things) and were — as many myths recounted — vulnerable to human foibles and passions..

Greek mythology does not just tell the stories of gods and goddesses, however. Human heroes including Hercules, the adventurer who performed 12 impossible labours for King Eurystheus (and was subsequently worshipped as a god for his accomplishment); Pandora, the first woman, whose curiosity brought evil to mankind; Pygmalion, the king who fell in love with an ivory statue; Arachne, the weaver who was turned into a spider for her arrogance; handsome Trojan prince Ganymede who became the cupbearer for the gods; Midas, the king with the golden touch; and Narcissus, the young man who fell in love with his own reflection are just as significant.

Monsters and "hybrids" (human-animal forms) also feature prominently in the tales: the winged horse Pegasus, the horse-man Centaur, the lion-woman Sphinx and the bird-woman Harpies, the one-eyed giant Cyclops, automatons (metal creatures given life by Hephaestus), manticores and unicorns, Gorgons, pygmies, minotaurs, satyrs and dragons of all sorts. Many of these creatures have become almost as well known as the gods, goddesses and heroes who share their stories…The characters, stories, themes and lessons of Greek mythology have shaped art and literature for thousands of years. They appear in Renaissance paintings such as Botticelli's Birth of Venus, Ruben's Triumph of Galatea and writings like Dante's Inferno; Romantic poetry and free-thinking literature; and scores of more recent novels, plays and movies.

One of the great benefits of myth is the healing process they show us, in that we are not alone with our feelings, fears, conflicts and aspirations. From Aboriginal folklore to Greek and Roman Gods, Norse heroes, native warriors- they all have a lesson to teach us. It goes without saying that myths, fairy tales, and fables to explain life's mysteries and to shed new light on them may help you and me on our own life journeys, be it just comfort and support in the legends of the past. The beliefs, myths, legends and folklore of the Greeks and Roman was learnt from the ancient Egyptians. We know of hundreds of gods and goddesses worshipped by the as their names, personalities and appearances have survived in the artwork the civilisation left behind. Throughout Egypt's history beliefs and practices were constantly changing though the themes of fertility, rebirth, death and resurrection generally remained constant. The ancient Egyptians had a tendency to merge new beliefs with the old ones rather than simply replace them. Akhenaten was a Pharaoh of the 18th dynasty of Egypt who ruled for 17 years. He is noted for being the first ruler to believe in one god, Aten, the solar disc, the deity of a strong monotheistic cult, and for his artistic innovations. When he introduced the rule of a 'One true God,' the Pharaoh then renamed himself Akhenaten ("servant of Aten") to show his dedication to this new God. Akhenaten was born around 1370 BC as Amenhotep IV. He was the son of Pharaoh Amenhotep III and Queen Tiye. Akhenaten's upbringing is not well-documented, but it is known that he was educated in religious texts and literature. He also received military training, as was customary for royal princes at the time. During his childhood, Egypt was the richest most powerful kingdom. Around the same time, Akhenaten outlawed the worship of all other gods in Egypt. He closed the temples of other deities, and he had their images removed from public places. This religious revolution was very controversial, and it was not well-received by the people of Egypt. Many felt that Akhenaten was betraying the traditions of their culture. There was also political unrest, as the powerful priests of Amun lost their influence. Akhenaten also moved the capital of Egypt from Thebes to a new city that he built, called Akhetaten ("Horizon of Aten"). The city was erected on a section of the Nile that had never been occupied before. He only erected temples dedicated to Aten there.

The wealth and prestige of a series of successful military Pharaohs had been shared with some powerful groups. The most powerful group at the time were the priests of Amun, who were based in the city of Thebes. The traditional idealised images of kings and gods were replaced by more realistic depictions of everyday life. This change is most evident in the artwork produced at Akhetaten, which depicts the royal family in a much more naturalistic style than had been seen before. This new art style may have been inspired by Akhenaten's belief that Aten was present in all things, including humans.

The sun disk of the Aten featured prominently in artwork from this time with arms outstretched, symbolising rays of light.
Akhenaten's reign was marked by conflict both within Egypt and beyond its borders. In domestic affairs, he faced opposition from the powerful priesthoods of other gods. The priests of Amun were particularly opposed to Akhenaten's religious revolution, but they were required to become priests in the new Aten religion and forget their old gods. Akhenaten was eventually succeeded by his probable son Tutankhamen. Akhenaten's religious revolution did not last long after his death. By the end of his reign, Akhenaten was unpopular with both the Egyptian people and the ruling class. His son Tutankhamun reverted back to the worship of Amun and reopened the temples of other gods. He even returned the capital city back to Thebes. It is likely that Tutankhamun felt he needed to undo his father's changes in order to regain the support of the people. After all, Akhenaten's reign was a time of great turmoil and conflict, both within Egypt and beyond its borders. Whilst the 'One true God' belief died to a great degree in the times of the Greek and Roman empires, it has of course remained with Jewish and biblical text of the coming of a Saviour as it has with Christian belief of a living Christ of Roman times who sacrificed himself for the defects of character of humanity in order that we all may be saved and enter into eternal life with our maker when we die.

* * * * * * * * * * * *

In 1951 Fulton Sheen became a titular bishop, and he served as auxiliary bishop of New York (1951–66). During much of his tenure in New York, he hosted a weekly television series, Life Is Worth Living (1951–57), that attracted about 30 million viewers. The following is an extract from one of his television broadcasts: [The first Greek word for love is eros, e-r-o-s. It simply means friendship and human love. Eros was that little Greek god that used to shoot arrows into the earth to make it fertile. Eros was not something that pushed us to an object. It was something that pulled us, it was attractive. For example, the love of a person, the love of art, the love of philosophy, the love of a good life. All that was eros.

To give you an example of that love, here is the engagement of G. K. Chesterton. All you married women will regret that your proposal was not in this language. Chesterton wrote to his future wife: "There are four great lamps of thanksgiving burning before me. The first: is that I was born out of the same earth as you. Two, I have tried to love everything in the universe as a remote preparation for loving you. Three, I have never run after strange women. You cannot understand how much this prepares a man for true love. Four, my life ends here. It has led me to you." That is eros.

I once asked a husband, what he would like to be if he could come back to earth two years after he died, and he said: "My wife's second husband."

Then came Freud. Freud changed eros into the erotic. Then eros meant sexy. And this then became the modern understanding of love. The Greeks never intended that that kind of love should so degenerate. And the new erotic love takes the fig leaf that once used to be put in Greek sculpture over the secret parts of man and woman, and it puts it over the face, so that the person is not loved, but only the experience. You drink the water, you forget the glass. And this is modern love, erotic.

Now we come to the second Greek word for love. You all know it, everyone. It is philia. You know philia because you know Philadelphia. Adelphi's in Greek is brother, philia is love. Hence, Philanthropic, philia, love, Anthropos, man: love of humanity. Philia is not a love of person to person. Philia is a love for all humanity, regardless of race, creed, or colour, simply because people are made in the image and likeness of God. That is philia. Now you will say: "But I can't like everyone." That's true. Because liking is in the emotions, in the feelings. But we can love everyone, because love is in the will, and it can be commanded. Hence our Blessed Lord said: "A new commandment I give you, that you love one another." You understand now the difference between liking and loving. I can make it a little clearer this way. I don't like chicken. Monsignor had chicken for dinner one day. But if you invited me to dinner, and you had only chicken, and you would have been very embarrassed if I didn't eat, I would eat the chicken. I would love it because I could command myself to eat it. That's the difference between liking and loving. We may not be able to like everyone, but we can love them, and we can get above our emotional attitudes.

I once asked a missionary in the Pacific islands what was the greatest virtue of the people. "Well," he said, "I can tell you the greatest virtue in terms of the greatest vice. It is the sin of kai-po, the sin of eating alone. They would go without food for three or four days until they found someone to share it with." That is Philia.

I told you about this friend of mine who was 14 years in a Communist prison, and he was so much beaten by the Communists that he developed lung trouble and tuberculosis, and was considered at one time the sickest man in the prison. A new prisoner was brought in, who hid in his heel a lump of sugar. He took the lump of sugar out of his heel in prison, and said to the other prisoners, "Who needs this most?" And they said: "Give it to Richard Wurmbrand." It was given to my friend, and he said, "I immediately thought of others who needed that sugar. I hadn't seen sugar in six years. But I put the sugar on the bed next to me." Two years later, that sugar had gone the rounds of all the prisoners and came back again to his bed. And then he started it on another round. Imagine all these victims of the Communist Persecution, in their adversity, being so devoted one to another.
About eight years ago I was on a plane, going from New York to Chicago, and as the plane took off, the stewardess sat down alongside me. She was a ravishingly beautiful girl. Celibacy doesn't blind us, you know. I can look at the menu without ordering.

She said, "Do you remember me?" I said, "No, I don't. I ought to, but I don't." She hesitated for a moment then continued "Well," she said, "Two years ago on this plane, I sat with you for 20 minutes, and I remember every word you said."

"Well, you began by saying: 'You are a very beautiful girl. Did you know that of all the gifts that God gives, the one that he gets back last and least of all, is the gift of beauty? He gives money; owners use it for the poor. He gives the gift of song, and people sing for his glory. But too often, when God gives beauty, he gets back nothing but a pile of old bones. So, inasmuch as you are so exceptionally endowed, why don't you give your beauty to people who have never seen anything beautiful?' That's what you said." She said: "I've had two years to think it over, and now I'm ready to do anything." I asked: "When?" and she said:"Now"

"All right. Come to my office, and I will tell you where you will go."She said, "Tell me now. I'm ready to go." "All right. You're going to a leper colony in Vietnam." So I sent her to a leper colony in Vietnam. She has a little jeep, drives around the villages and searches, particularly under bridges, because when lepers are driven out of the villages, they hide under the bridges. And then she takes them to a leprosarium, where a doctor cares for these people. In one of her letters, she said: "I do not know whether they ever think that they are ever looking at anything beautiful, but I know that I am: the gratitude of these good people." This is philia, the second kind of love. And now we come to the third Greek word. And there is no English equivalent for this, so you have to learn the word: A-G-A-P-E: *ágape*. It was used before Christ, but never with any fixed meaning. But when a new love came to this earth, the love of God for man, the word *eros* would not do. The word *philia* would not do. So the Holy Spirit inspired the New Testament writers to seek some other word that would express this abounding, boundless love of God for man. And they hit upon the word *agape* (in the verb form). And it is used 250 times in the New Testament. If you went into the original Greek, you would find that this word was *agape*, love. Pick up the 13th chapter of St. Paul's first letter to the Corinthians. The whole 13th chapter is on love. It's the most beautiful passage on love in the world. And the Greek word is the one I gave you. You see, we had to have a new word. The world had never thought of sacrificial love. It's easy to love those who love you, as Our Lord said. But to love when you're unloved that's heroic. God loves me. Now I am not particularly loveable. And God loves you. Now two or three of you will admit, too, that you are not particularly loveable either. But God loves you anyway. Why does he love you? Why does he love me? He puts his love into us; that's why. Therefore we become loveable. A mother, for example, will put her love into a child, regardless of what that child is, whether useful or not. So God puts his love into us. To give you an example of what this love is like because it is so unearthly, suppose a lifeguard at a beach is asked, "If there was a very beautiful girl drowning out there in the surf, would you risk your life to save her?" He very likely would say, "Yes, I would, particularly if she's very beautiful, I would risk my life." "Or suppose there's a person out there drowning in the surf who did you and your family a lot of harm. Would you rescue that person?" He would think about it. Now that is the way God loved us when we were unlovable, when we were his enemies He loved us. We have been guilty of the death of Christ. We nailed him to that cross. As I look at him, I see my own sins and life. I am guilty of that death. And on Easter Sunday morning when he arises from the dead, I can say, "See, he's alive. I'm free." That is the meaning of agape: love.   Now come back to what I said at the beginning. Is it true now, that anything is all right, provided you love? No. What kind of love? Eros? Erotic? Philia? Agape? And this is the love to which we are committed not just a sentimental love, but the love for the unlovable, to those who are anti-love.]

Agape- love is a spiritual quest that has provided one of the greatest themes of literature and art for over a millennium, for there is something irrepressible within the human soul that never ceases to aspire to something greater than itself, nor does it ever relinquish its belief that something eternal survives beyond the death of the mortal body. This is perhaps the greatest difference between us and the other animals with whom we share this planet.

CHAPTER 2.

THE SPIRITUAL QUEST

This quest is more than just a desire to serve God; it involves a search for knowledge- not only knowledge of the divine couched in traditional religious belief, myth and folklore but also in the kind of knowledge of the laws underpinning reality that the world greatest scientists and psychologists pursue and that the everyday ordinary man aspires too. The quest for knowledge may take us down dark paths, as well as those lit by sunlight, and may reveal to us the evil that lay within us, as within our defects of character, as equally as the goodness within our heart and higher soul self.

So before I traverse the ladder to the kingdom that lies within, as shown in the life reality or myth of He (The One) who reportedly sacrifices himself for mankind, there are but three mythical stories I seek to relate here which deal with spiritual quests. All three involve self confrontation which throws a sharp relief of the deep paradox of dark and light which lies at the core of the human soul.

The mysterious battle between good and evil within the human soul is displayed nowhere better than in the mythical story of Dr. Faustus. This mythical medieval great tragedy of Dr. Faustus from the pen of Christopher Marlowe (1564-1593) and that of Johann Wolfgang von Goeth's (1749-1831) epic poem of Faust, a two-part dramatic work of the 18th century of which both stories tells the tale of a man whose spiritual quest ultimately led him to sell his soul to the devil. His eventual recognition of his egocentricity for recognition from his peers and the rewards of earthly pleasures are but a shadow of the higher power self which finally brings him to remorse and compassion. It is indeed a powerful image of the need to comprehend the dark and the light in order to find peace.

In the story, Dr. Faustus is a brilliant philosopher and student of theology whose studies offered about the nature of God and the meaning of life do not satisfy his enquiring mind. He secretly seeks to uncover the answers without the assistance of any other intellectuals of his time as he wishes to obtain all the credit for his future findings. The nature of his egocentricity is much like any man who has overlooked that the ego is like a grain of sand upon the beach that can sometimes think it is the beach. It has its small part in the scheme of things but is not the whole. He allows his mind's ego to drift into dark places in search of his quest, thus hypothetically his ego thinks of itself like the whole beach- the puffed-up mindset of anyone intent on self-infused gratification for recognition in the future. In his ego delusion, Faustus abandons his theology and becomes a student of hermetic magic, hoping to find life's secrets in alchemical experiments and the forbidden knowledge of magic and sorcery passed down through the ages by ancient Egyptians. Yet even these forbidden researches could not teach him all he wished to know, and he sank into a deep despondency. In desperation, he called upon the infernal spirits and summoned the power of Lucifer and his dark angels for guidance. In a very short period of time, a mysterious dog appeared in his study which metamorphosed into a strange figure who announced himself to be Mephistopheles, the spirit of evil and affirmation. Lucifer had given Mephistopheles the task to be forever on the lookout for human souls whom he could win over to the darkness, thus cheating God, and Faustus, who in desperation wanted the knowledge of life's secrets and divine nature accepted the pact of Mephistopheles by signing away his life in a blood oath to the devil's angel, on the condition that Faustus would be Mephistopheles servant here on this earth. He unknowingly sold away his immortal soul until eternity.

For a time Faustus was excited by the magic and mysteries shown him by the evil one and believed he was at last getting close to the knowledge and secrets of God. But the dark spirit of his negation gradually eroded the scholars' will and lured him into deeper and deeper sensuality and pride, and a sense of spiritual quest was lost. It was contrived by Mephistopheles to lure Faustus into a lust-filled relationship with a young girl called Gretchen, and when she became pregnant by Faustus he abandoned her. Gretchen went mad and killed the infant child in despair, and was then executed for her crime. It was then that Faustus realised the terrible destruction he had wrought on innocent human life and suffered deep and bitter remorse, for although he was bound to Mephistopheles' will, he had begun to truly love the girl, thus something in his soul was kept free of corruption. And this Mephistopheles had not anticipated, since the redemptive power of love was not something in the spirit of negation and he had no knowledge of. However, the power Mephistopheles had over Faustus caused the philosopher to indulge in every sexual pleasure imaginable to man and he penetrated every secret mystery, for many years. All that he had wanted to know he had learnt; and he understood the glorious heights of heaven and shrouded depth of the underworld. However the remorse of losing Gretchen grew like cancer inside of him, and in spite of his corruption, something inside of him longed for the light. As Faustus grew older Mephistopheles waited with patience and satisfaction that the time was near for the scholar to face death, his soul as agreed signed over in a blood oath meant that his soul would belong to the darkness for eternity. But at the last moment, as Faustus faced the truth of the pact he had made, and he was so filled with remorse and love, that his suffering soul slipped from the grasp of Mephistopheles and the scholar-philosopher was born again to the light and the heavenly kingdom.

Faustus' story is a mythic metaphor for every human being's struggle to find the light in the midst of darkness. Faustus is the paradigm of the inner world of all of us, full of conflict egocentric desires and longing to serve something lighter and greater than ourselves. Although Faustus had its roots in medieval Christianity and therefore presents good and evil in a somewhat simplistic way, nevertheless the message transcends any specific religious doctrine, particularly if it's understood psychologically from the conflict within our nature. Faustus is symbolic of the questing spirit within each and every human being, which is courageous enough to reject the dogma of any religious faith in preference to the spirituality that lay within. Yet it can be dangerously arrogant to assume that it can defy fundamental human morality in the name of knowledge. We may well condemn Faustus for his greed and arrogance but still admire him for the courage of his convictions and willingness to risk his soul in order to penetrate the hearts of life's mysteries. Herein we are presented with the paradox of good and evil, for in order to truly understand the former, we must recognise the latter; and in order to make that recognition, we must meet it first in the secret darkness of our own hearts. The spiritual quest, if it is truly heartfelt, arises not from childlike acceptance of belief, but from the disillusionment and profound desire to understand life's paradoxes.

To tread that path of spiritual enlightenment we must venture past the childlike faith of our former life and be willing to be ever mindful of the God of our own understanding guidance with both love and equally an element of remorse. We may well have to step forth and be led through darkness and destruction of the faith of our Father's holy faith, and perhaps feeling for a time that we are irredeemable our own pact, so to speak with the devil with our nature, being our own defects of character, to come to the grace imposed on us by God for our salvation, like Faustus. Grace is a term much broader than the term of Christianity, it is an inner mysterious release that arises from within, which makes us sense not only the goodness but our evil as well. It is then that we must listen to God for guidance and be with God to carry out the being in this world but not of it. It is the grace we receive by good orderly direction that God guides through our prayer. It is the mindfulness of our defects of pride, covertness, lust, anger, gluttony, envy and sloth that we need to overcome and understand the darkness of our nature as equally as the light talent we must act upon. The inner journey is a personal mystery of two sides of the same coin which reflects the two dimensions of the human being. We must learn to use our defects for good as equally as we are conscious of the darkness that sometimes entraps us with them. It is through the agency of our inner darkness that we may eventually find our way to the light.

There is a mythical belief in a wheel of rebirth to a state of Enlightenment. We see in the life of Siddhartha Buddha a man who left his place of luxury and pleasure as a young man to pursue his destiny. We see him through struggle and suffering and begin to understand the meaning of life. The Buddha's enlightenment may be taken here as an actual event, a religious parable or a myth in the most profound psychological sense one may find truth in all three interpretations. As a myth, the tale presents us with a paradigm of every human soul's journey from the darkness of ignorance to a transformative comprehension of the cycle of life and death.

During what has been called the second urbanisation of north-eastern India, emerging small kingdoms caused upheaval in all areas: economic, social and religious. Brahmin priests no longer retained the level of prestige and power they had as Vedic rituals and religious traditions lost their value, and more people turned their focus inward. They sought to know the true nature of reality that was at the basis of religious practice and the very foundation of life. Men and women of all castes gave up everything to live a life of meditation, yoga, contemplation, starvation, self-mortification and deprivation of all kinds, in order to find this freedom, self-knowledge and fulfilment. Known as *Samanas*, there were so many of them that they were regarded as a fifth caste.

These ascetics and sages lived alone in caves or forests, or with their families in communities. They were supported by those who felt unable to do the same but who, by helping them, believed that they gained Karmic benefits.

Siddhartha Gotama (490-410 BC), legend has it, was a royal Prince whose father had protected him from any kind of suffering. From the time of his birth until the age of 29, he was given everything that one could possibly want: looks and riches, a beautiful wife, and a healthy son. Then, at 29 he encountered sickness, old age, and death for the first time. Overcome by what he saw, Gotama recognised that all beings were subject to these things, no matter how much they had of worldly goods and splendour. He could no longer ignore the realities of life: suffering and death. Then he met a Samana who had renounced everything but appeared happy nonetheless, so, following his example, he left his home forever, and took up the begging bowl and staff of the Samana, to seek the end of his *samsara,* the constant cycle of births, deaths and rebirths. Tradition refers to this episode as the 'Four Sights .'

For six years Gotama practised the ascetic arts, travelling throughout the cities of the Ganges basin, studying with teachers who could impart the disciplines that would end his samsara. He learned yogic meditation and other practices but refused to believe that the temporary states arrived at was the highest realisation possible to man. He deprived himself of food until he became emaciated, but concluded that this method only intensified suffering, it did not release one from it. Siddhartha knew that he must get beyond asceticism, just as he had got beyond a worldly life. He had reached a stage of exhaustion and was as thin as a skeleton. It was then he accepted a bowl of rice offered to him by a village girl who was moved with compassion by his weakness. He then bathed in a river and was abandoned by his five disciples who had shared his austerities. They saw him then as self-indulgent and that perhaps he was not so enlightened as they had previously thought him to be.

He realised that neither the pleasures of life nor the ascetic practices of the Samana offered him the wisdom he sought. He needed to find a way between these two extremes – this he called the *Middle Way.*

Siddhartha then started for a place called Buddha-Gaya, where he might find the Tree of Wisdom. As he passed through a forest, so much light emanated from his body that birds were attracted and flew in circles around him. And the animals of the forest escorted him to the sacred fig tree. He sat a bundle of new-mown hay down and sat on it, then uttered a vow: "Here on this seat, may my body stay and dry up, my skin and flesh waste away, for before I rise up I will have attained the knowledge I seek!"Siddhartha remained unmoved in heart and appearance, calm as a lotus flower on still water. He was tempted many times, but the demon's daughters retired defeated. Then Lucifer sent an army of horrible devils who surrounded the fig tree and threatened Siddhartha. So profound was Siddhartha's serenity that they found themselves paralysed, with their arms bound to their sides.

Finally, the demon Mara rode down from the clouds and hurled his weapon- a huge disk that could cut a mountain in two. But this weapon was impotent against Siddhartha. It was then changed into a garland of flowers and hung suspended above Siddhartha's head. The demon was finally beaten. The motionless Siddhartha remained in meditation under the sacred fig tree. Night came, and with it, enlightenment slowly rose in his heart. First, he knew the exact conditions of living for all beings, and then the causes of their rebirth into the world of form. Throughout all ages, he beheld sentient beings live, die and be reincarnated. He remembered his own previous existence and grasped the inevitable links of cause and effect. As he meditated on human suffering he was enlightened as to how it came about and the means which might allow it to cease. When the dawn came Siddhartha had achieved perfect enlightenment and had become a Buddha. He continued meditation for seven days then remained near the sacred tree for another four weeks. For the rest of his life, he laboured to teach men and women the mystery of suffering and rebirth. Buddha did not want his teaching to be accepted by his authority. Anything can become an object of attachment, even his own teaching. He encouraged the individual to take responsibility for his own beliefs. For the Buddha karma was rooted in *intentional* acts, it was not absolute as in the Hindu conception. He advised that pupils should not accept anything simply because it is traditional or hearsay; or because it comes from a sacred text, because it seems rational, logical, or comes from a teacher who is competent, or charismatic. He emphasised that one should check one's views, test ideas and guard against the possibility of bias. Buddha emphasised spiritual self-sufficiency and responsibility, rather than depending upon the Brahmin priests. He taught that spiritual attainment was no longer limited to certain castes, but possible for everyone, without discrimination based on gender, age, social status, or moral standing. He saw himself as a healer, not a god. He was never represented in human form until 300–400 years after death. When asked how he should be described, the Buddha said *"Remember me as one who is awake."*

Unlike his teachers, whose practices focused on achieving extra-sensory perceptions of the mind, Buddha-Gautama's emphasis was on the quality of "mindfulness" – awareness, without judgment, of mind, body and the environment. He remembered that as a child he had meditated and focused on his breath and that this had brought him a sense of both pervading calmness and awareness. He undertook a long and arduous period of meditation and contemplation that culminated in his acquiring deep insights into the human condition. Finally, in overcoming the temptations of the demonic Mara, he believed he did attain *Nibbana* (or *nirvana*) – the understanding that liberated him from samsara.

"In that instance, the knowledge and the vision arose in me, unshakable is the realisation in my mind, this is my last birth," At this moment he earned the title Buddha – the "Awakened One."

For 49 days, we are told, he enjoyed this liberation and pondered whether he could teach others how to attain it. Finally, he travelled on foot to Benares to seek the five ascetics who had deserted him when he gave up the samsara way. They recognised that something had changed in him, and, following his *Dhamma* (*Dharma*: teachings), became the first insight of Buddhism. Buddha taught for several decades throughout the cities of the Gangetic basin, building a community of followers. In 410 BCE, at the age of 80, he became mortally ill, his last words, tradition has it being: *"All compounded things are subject to decay, work out your salvation with diligence."* Hamma or the teachings of the Buddha the truth that leads to liberation.

1. Life is suffering (*Dukkha*) – our desires and expectations do not conform to the reality of the world, which is in a constant state of flux (*Anicca*), so we experience Dukkha.

2. The origin of suffering is attachment – not only do we fail to know reality but we *miss-know* it. We attribute permanence to impermanence. The physical universe is constant change, but we know it as permanent – *change is the only thing there is*. Our ideas, the objects that surround us, and our perceptions, are all transient. Even our idea of "self" is a delusion since there is no permanent self. *Craving* and *clinging* to these inevitably leads to suffering.

3. It is possible to end suffering in this life – Like the *moksha* in Hinduism, nibbana can be realised in life, through discipline and effort. Nibbana means freedom from troubles, worries, ideas, and the annihilation of the illusion of the self where one understands *Dhamma* – the Buddha's teaching and becomes an arahant.(i.e. one who has gained in sight into the true nature of existence.

4. The path to the cessation of suffering – The Middle Way – is a path between the extremes of clinging and aversion, both expressions of attachment, arriving at a state of complete equanimity. It is achieved through the Eightfold Path - *Summa* – "right," or that which promotes the end of suffering has traditionally been divided into three sections:

1. Right Understanding – a person becomes acquainted with the basic principles of *Dhamma*, the Buddha's teachings, and enters the path, gradually awakening an understanding of the wisdom he or she can attain at the end.

2. Right Intention – One contemplates the desire for all beings to be happy and free from suffering. One cultivates goodwill, harmlessness and non-attachment, avoiding tendencies towards greed, hatred and harm.

3. Right Speech – I will refrain from false speech – not only lying or slandering, but gossip, cursing, swearing or meaningless babble. I will communicate in kind, gentle and direct speech.

4. Right Action –There are 5 precepts of non-harming (*ahimsa*) – These are ideals that one vows to live by, to refrain from harming sentient beings; to refrain from taking what is not offered; to refrain from sexual misconduct; to refrain from false speech; to refrain from alcohol.

5. Right Livelihood – to earn a living in a way that benefits humanity.Disciplining the Mind. By "Mind" the Buddha meant the totality of thoughts, sensations, feelings and consciousness that are experienced at each moment. The mind has great potential, but the undeveloped mind is like a wild horse: difficult to stay attentive, it craves stimulation, jumping from thought to thought, dwelling in the past or in the future, with thoughts that often cause anxiety or fear. When this undisciplined mind does pay attention to the present, it does so with opinions and emotional reactions rather than *being* in the present. To bring the mind under control is necessary, but it requires patience, skill, and persistent training.   6.

Right Effort –Since deluded thinking hinders the ability to understand the world, the student pays deliberate attention to developing positive thoughts that alleviate suffering and let go of negative ones, he or she practices generosity and patience.

7. Right Mindfulness takes meditative awareness into everyday life. Doing so can restrain the mind's proclivity to make judgments, and reduce its tendency to need stimulation.

8. Right Concentration – Take time daily to practice meditative awareness.

These eight elements are symbolised by a wheel and are to be practised simultaneously since the practice of one supports the practice of the others. The Buddha maintained that one could develop the virtues described as one would develop any skill, with regular practice. This story is an example of his teaching: "Once there was a woman named Kisagotami, whose only son died. With the dead child in her arms, she ran from house to house begging, "Please give me medicine for my son." Seeing her, the people shook their heads in pity. "Poor Kisagotami, you have lost your senses. Your son is dead. He is beyond the help of medicine." She, however, refused to accept this and went on wandering in the streets asking everyone she met for help. A gentle old man took pity on her and said, "Go to the Buddha. He will help you." In haste, Kisagotami took her dead son to the Buddha and asked, "Is there a medicine to cure my son?" He looked at the closed eyes of the child and understood, "I will heal your son if you bring me a handful of mustard seed." Joyfully, Kisagotami started off to get them. Then the Buddha added, "But the seeds must come from a house where no one has died." Kisagotami went to every house in the city and asked for the mustard seed. "We have plenty of mustard seeds," everyone said. "Take all that you need." Then she asked, "Has anyone ever died in this house?" "But of course," she was told. "There have been many deaths here." "I lost my father," "I lost my sister," "I lost my daughter." "There are more dead here than living." She could not find one house that had not been visited by death. Weary and with all hope gone, Kisagotami sat on a hilltop and watched the fires of the city flicker up and die out. Suddenly she came to her senses and said, "The lives of people flicker up and go out like fire. My son is not the only one who has died. Everyone dies. How selfish I am in my grief!" She buried her son amid the wildflowers and returned to the Buddha, "Now

I understand your teaching," she said, holding out an empty hand. Kisagotami joined the *sanga* (community) and became insightful.

"The great symbol of the Tree of Wisdom, under which Siddhartha achieved enlightenment, echoes the images of many other myths. The Tree of Knowledge may be found in the biblical story of Adam and Eve in the garden of Eden; the Tree of Immortality lies at the bottom of the sea, beckoning Gilgamesh in the Babylonian myth, and the World-Tree holds up the cosmos in Norse and Teutonic myth. For millennia the human imagination has envisaged the source of life and wisdom as a tree, perhaps because the tree portrays the fundamental duality that lies at the core of the human soul. And as it is a living thing, not an intellectual construction, the spiritual truths that Siddhartha seeks can be found only through such contact with organic life.

The demon Mara, viewed psychologically, is a dimension of Siddhartha himself. Like Mephistopheles in the story of Faustus, he is the personification of inner darkness and attempts to corrupt Siddhartha in the same way that Mephistopheles corrupts Faustus. But, unlike Faustus, Siddhartha's absolute serenity reflects his total commitment to his quest. It is an issue of focus and commitment to the priorities of giving central importance to the mysteries he is contemplating. We will find no inner serenity if we are constantly distracted by our own internal demons, be they physical temptations, or fear and anxieties. Inner focus is not the same as rigid asceticism; it is an attitude, a state of mind, rather than a prescribed set of disciplines. And perhaps this is why the Buddha alone could focus on the important issues of the inner world. The intense inner effort of this kind may indeed only be possible in the second half of our life, when we are weary with satiation, and the suffering of others begins to mean more to us than our own small worldly pleasures and pains.

CHAPTER 3.

FINDING THE INNER GRAIL

The stages through which Siddhartha passes are stages of life experience, each of which is necessary for him to move into the next stage. He must try everything before he is ready to relinquish everything for what he is seeking. We may not be able to achieve the kind of enlightenment described in the story of Buddha; it may even be arrogant to try. Whether perceived as a mythic image or a great religious avatar, the Buddha is a paradigm rather than an ordinary mortal. However, understanding our lives from a larger perspective, with an awareness of the cause and effect that lies behind so much human suffering, may be possible for all of us- if we are prepared to quietly and unobtrusively place our quest for understanding at the centre of our lives.

In English history, we read of many knights of the realm who worshipped their king and fought to the death for the cause of the King and Kingdom. In the mythical kingdom of Camelot According to the most widely accepted version of the legend, the Knights of the Round Table were a group of brave warriors who pledged to defend the kingdom of Camelot and uphold the values of chivalry. They were led by King Arthur, a legendary figure who is said to have ruled Britain in the 5th or 6th century.

The story of Parsifal is part of the medieval legend of King Arthur and the Quest for the Holy Grail. The Grail myth dates back to at least the twelfth century in Europe and was transmitted in various versions, including French (from the poet Chretien de Troyes), English (Le Morte D'arthur, by Thomas Malory), German (Wolfram von Eschenbach's version, which became the basis for Richard Wagner's "Parsifal" opera) and others. The Grail myth speaks directly to our psyche, and in particular, as the great Jungian analyst Robert A. Johnson notes in his seminal work, "He," to the development of the psychology of the masculine, in both men and women – and it is as relevant now as it has ever been.

The myth surrounds the wounded Fisher King, Amfortas, the king of the Grail castle. He is in agonising pain, and the kingdom suffers as a result. The Fisher King wound, in psychological terms, is a common condition for Western Man, where every young man, as Johnson notes, *"has naively blundered into something that is too big for him. He proceeds halfway through his masculine development and then drops it as being too hot. Often a certain bitterness arises, because, like the Fisher King, he can neither live with the new consciousness he has touched nor can he entirely drop it."* This wound, however, is crucial for the development of consciousness, for its redemption, through the intercession of Parsifal, is what leads to the complete integration of the Self – it is what leads to a life of self-awareness, contentment, passion and authenticity. The court jester explains that the Fisher King could only be healed through the actions of an innocent fool, who would spontaneously need to ask a specific question. As Johnson again so eloquently explains, *"A man must consent to look to a foolish, innocent, adolescent part of himself for his cure. The inner fool is the only one who can touch his Fisher King wound."*

Enter Parsifal, a name which means "pure fool," an innocent young man raised by his overly-protective mother in poverty, knowing nothing of his dead father (who himself was a knight), without any direction or schooling. He is dazzled one day by the appearance of a group of knights who visit his village and, to his mother's dismay, decides with all the bluster of youth to seek them out to become a knight himself. She agrees to let him go, but gives him a homespun garment that he elects to wear for much of his life; this garment, Johnson notes, represents the "Mother Complex" in psychology, and will prove costly to Parsifal in his development.

Parsifal finds and enters Arthur's Court but is initially ridiculed and expelled; however, legend held that a damsel in Arthur's Court who had not smiled for years would burst into laughter at the sight of the greatest knight – which she did at the sight of innocent Parsifal. The Court immediately held Parsifal in high regard and Arthur knighted him on the spot. Parsifal, naive and not burdened with fear or anxiety, seeks out the most fearsome knight of all, the Red Knight, a warrior so fierce he had never been defeated. Parsifal, in his earnest naïveté, confronts him and asks him for his horse and armour. Laughing, he agrees, but only if Parsifal can take it. Predictably, Parsifal is knocked to the ground by the powerful knight but, as he falls, Parsifal throws his dagger into the Red Knight's eye, killing him. This victory, as Robert Johnson surmises, represents the integration of the *"shadow side of masculinity, the negative, potentially destructive power . . . [he] must not repress his aggressiveness since he needs the masculine power of his Red Knight shadow to make his way through the mature world."* The newly empowered knight goes out seeking battle and adventure, rescuing maidens and defeating opponents, but not killing them; any knight Parsifal overcame he instead had then swear allegiance to the King.

One day along his heroic quest, Parsifal sought lodging but was told there was no place to stay for miles. He then encounters a man fishing in a boat on a lake and asks if he knows of any place to stay for the night. The fisherman, the Fisher King, tells him to go down the road a little bit and go left. Parsifal obliges and suddenly finds himself on the grounds of the Grail Castle, windows gleaming, knights and ladies greeting him, the splendour of which he had never dreamed of in his life. A great ceremony was about to begin, one which occurred every evening. A great feast and celebration was held where maidens brought out to all assembled the Holy Grail, from which all would partake, immediately granting them whatever they desired – everyone, that is, except for the Fisher King. Because of his agonising wound, he was unable to drink from the Grail, and his affliction continued to wreak havoc across the kingdom. During his quest, Parsifal had encountered a mentor, Gourmand, who had instructed him in the ways of knighthood. When encountering the Holy Grail, Gourmand instructed Parsifal to ask an important question, "Whom does the Grail serve?" This was the question that would heal the Grail King's wound. However, his mother had also told him not to ask too many questions and hers was the advice Parsifal heeded this time in the Great Hall. All assembled knew the prophecy that one day an innocent fool would enter the castle and ask the question that would heal the King – all except Parsifal – and very quickly the ceremony ended, with everyone retiring for the night. The next morning, Parsifal rides out and the Grail Castle disappears. This loss tormented Parsifal, and it would take years of gruelling, rigorous battles and quests before Parsifal realised that the homespun garment that he wore beneath his armour – the psychological symbol of the Mother Complex – had to be removed before he could partake of the Grail and heal the Fisher King. Parsifal spends some twenty years earning his way back to the Grail Castle. They are difficult years, however, and he grows in bitterness and disillusionment; these represent the difficult years of middle age, where one begins to question one's very existence and the choices made. After twenty years of searching in vain for what was lost in his first encounter at the Grail Castle, Parsifal has had his arrogance and pride beaten and humbled. One day, along his latest quest, he is introduced to a forest hermit. At first, the hermit scolds him for his failures – especially for not asking the question when he first encountered the Fisher King. However, he soon softens, sympathising with Parsifal, and invites him to go down the road a little bit and go to the left. Again, Parsifal suddenly finds himself on the grounds of the Grail Castle, this time, however, with twenty long years of earned experience and humility.

Again, he finds himself in the midst of the great feast and celebration where maidens bring out the Holy Grail for all to partake. This time, however, Parsifal asks the question, "Whom does the Grail serve?" The simple act of asking the question immediately heals the Grail King and the entire Castle erupts in celebration! What is the answer to the question? "You, My Lord, are the Grail King." "And what exactly does this answer mean? Very simply, we serve something far greater than ourselves." Carl Jung,

"One can not pursue happiness; if he does he obscures it. If he will proceed with the human task of life, the relocation of the centre of gravity of the personality to something greater outside itself, happiness will be the outcome."

The myth of the Grail has been interpreted on many different levels over centuries, and all of them have some truth. From a psychological perspective, it is an inner journey, and although the imagery of the original story is Christian, the inner journey is compatible with any deep religious faith, orthodox or unorthodox. It is really a journey of compassion, which can only occur if we allow ourselves to feel with others and suffer the consequences of our own actions. It is the compassion that allows Parsifal to respond in the right way to the sick king, and it is in compassion that allows all of us to see beyond our own concerns to the wasteland around all humans to find some small ray of light to illuminate their mortal journey. The sick king and the Grail are images within Parsifal himself, as they are within us all. The king represents the spiritual sickness of the meaningless, the Grail is the overflowing cup of unity with the interest of life which is the only antidote to meaninglessness. Religion has many terminologies for compassion, but in reality, perhaps these are unnecessary for most transformative experiences that arise from that mysterious sense of uni-

ty that can only occur when we share another's pain and joy. This is the crux of Parsifal's myth. The sick king is healed at the end of the story, but the epilogue continues... For once healed the king willingly accepts death so that his crown may pass on to his grandson. Herein lay the mythical story of another presentation of death as a symbol of transformation. That which is injured may now heal and pass away and thus is renewal and fullness of hope that may govern the motives by which we l		i		v		e		.
Thus the suffering that we experience in life, which seems to be so irrevocably wounding, may be relinquished so that life can begin again in a spirit of renewal of gratitude, hope and generosity to others. It is right and fitting that Parsifal in his youth made mistakes and was foolish. It is also right and fitting that as he grew older he gradually experienced increasing weariness and cynicism; the spiritual quest beginning to replace his earlier determination to be a great knight and receive recognition in the outer world. Thus we may well ask, at a certain point when we grow weary of accumulation of possessions, or striving for worldly success, what purpose our lives truly serve. There is eventually a realisation that whatever our skills, efforts, aspirations and actions in life, death comes to us all. Be we strong or weak, clever or ignorant, wealthy or poor, good or evil, we must eventually bow to the great leveller. Death is the only absolute constant in life, and yet remains life's greatest enigma- for no matter how we become, we cannot solve the mystery of what happens to us when the body dies. So whatever our station in life, our skills, efforts, aspirations and actions in life, death comes to us all. Be we strong or weak. Clever or ignorant, wealthy or poor, good or evil, we must all eventually bow to the great leveller. Death is the only absolute constant in life, and yet remains life's greatest enigma-

for no matter how scientifically sophisticated we may become, we cannot solve the mystery of what happens to us when the body dies. Human beings have long believed that something survives beyond the physical shell. Myths have always been expressed in our imaginations from our human fears, fantasies and expectations of death. Religions have always attempted to offer certainties about the afterlife, teaching us that our adherence to particular dogmas during our lives will guarantee favourable conditions after death. myth offers answers, all that remains for us is the profound paradox of death, which combines the transient nature of mortal life with the eternal and indestructible; nature of the greater life of which we are part.

In the Bible, there is the story of Ecclesiastes, which shows us in stunning ways that the key to life is not in life itself. Pleasure, materialism, wisdom, and money are all futile and folly. True happiness comes from centring our lives on God, not ourselves.

Everything is ordered in time and people are subject to time in contrast to God's eternal character. The world is filled with injustice, which only God will adjudicate. God and humans do not belong in the same realm, and it is therefore necessary to have the right attitude before God. Ecclesiastes describes the meaninglessness of living without God. We see that God created the world and called it "good." But despite this original goodness, humanity fell into sin, and all creation was subjected to the curse of God. This brought into the world meaninglessness, violence, and frustration. The theme of Ecclesiastes is the necessity of fearing God in this fallen, confusing world. " Each human being wants to understand all the ways God is acting in the world, but he cannot, because he is not God. And yet the faithful do not despair but cling to God, even when they cannot see what God is doing. Everything is meaningless." What does man gain from all his labour at which he toils under the sun? Generations come and generations go, but the earth remains forever."

The book of Ecclesiastes is unique and provocative as it states powerfully and repeatedly that everything is meaningless ("vanity") without a proper focus on God. The book reveals the necessity of fearing God in a fallen and frequently confusing and frustrating world.
Ecclesiastes guides us to the real truth behind all things: putting our fear, love, and trust in God alone. Solomon's wisdom teaches us that life is long and difficult and that much of our time is spent on vanity. He is not inviting us to despise our lives, our work, our possessions, or the pleasures in life.
People ought to enjoy every day of their lives, no matter how long they live. But they should also remember this: You will be dead for a long time. Everything that happens then is useless. Young people, enjoy yourselves while you are young; be happy while you are young. Every man also to whom God hath given riches and wealth, and hath given him the power to eat thereof, and to take his portion, and to rejoice in his labour—this is the gift of God. Life only has meaning when living in a relationship with God.
Solomon wants his readers to know that he has tried everything in a relentless pursuit to find the meaning of life. He's tried gaining knowledge and wisdom and being very righteous. Now all has been heard; here is the conclusion of the matter: Fear God and keep his commandments, for this is the whole [duty] of man. For God will bring every deed into judgment, including every hidden thing, whether it is good or evil. It is quite simply meaningless. Yet we know, and part of the point of the book of

Ecclesiastes in the Bible is to show us that life is not meaningless when it is centred around God and enjoying the God who gives good gifts for us to enjoy. "Vanity of vanities! All is vanity." People never get anywhere from all their hard work

."For everything there is a season, and a time for every matter under heaven: a time to be born, and a time to die; a time to plant, and a time to pluck up what is planted; a time to kill, and a time to heal; a time to break down, and a time to build up; a time to weep, and a time to laugh; a time to mourn, and a time to dance; a time to throw away stones, and a time to gather stones together; a time to embrace, and a time to refrain from embracing; a time to seek, and a time to lose; a time to keep, and a time to throw away; a time to tear, and a time to sew; a time to keep silence, and a time to speak; and a time to love, a time to hate, a time to war, and a time of peace (Ecclesiastes 3:1)

My sympathies as you move through this rich process of both celebrating a life well lived, and grieving at the transition of death. Ecclesiastes is the work of a Teacher who lived and wrote in Jerusalem sometime after 450 BCE—after the Hebrews returned from Exile in Babylon. It's a time in which, according to the Teacher, people are allowing concerns about human existence to become more important than spiritual commitment—and, conversely, using their religious faith simply as a way of improving their human lives.

CHAPTER 4.

THE PLAY OF UNENDING LIFE

"Vanity of vanities, all is vanity," Ecclesiastes begins (1:2), and in this familiar passage, he affirms a universal Truth that remains constant through all the conflicting experiences life might offer. Metaphysically, it's interesting to note that this passage consists of seven sets, each with two pairs of opposites. From the opening pages of Genesis (and its seven days of creation) through the multiple sevens we find in the closing Revelation to John, the Bible recognises that there are seven stages involved in the process of expressing our spiritual truth in this human experience. Each stage is represented by two sets of opposites. The first stage involves birth and death, planting and reaping—the basics of coming into this human experience through one gate and leaving through another. The second stage involves killing, healing, breaking down and building up—a step of learning how this dualistic experience works. The third stage is weeping and laughing, mourning and dancing—incorporating our feeling nature into the physical experience. Fourth—throwing away stones and gathering stones, embracing and refraining from embracing—centres us in our heart chakra, teaching that love is not just gathering, but also releasing. In the fifth stage we seek and lose, keep and throw away—this is the power centre, in which we begin to take ownership of our lives. The sixth stage involves tearing and sewing, silence and speaking—opposites involved in creating new possibilities by claiming our spiritual truth ("speaking the word"). And the final opposites involve love and hate, war and peace. The important point, I think, is that both ends of each spectrum are intimately involved in the creative process we are here to accomplish. We embrace healing, dancing, embracing and love. We often judge ourselves negatively if we find ourselves experiencing death and weeping and losing and war. But to judge one extreme as "good" and the other as "bad" is to miss the essential point that the whole spectrum must be involved if we are to achieve the kingdom of heaven.

We can and will overcome the fear of death and live in accord with our maker if we meditate upon it. The great mystery of faith is that love is to be found in our hearts if only we can be silent and still if we can make this love the supreme centre of our being. That means turning to it wholeheartedly and paying attention to it. You approach your life with love because what you encounter in your own heart is the living principle of love. Listen to St.Paul suggest how we should be in our relationship with one another. 'Bear with one another and, if anyone has a complaint against another, forgive each other as the Lord forgives you. Above all, clothe yourself with love, as the Lord binds reverting together in perfect harmony.' (Cor.3:13-15). The most important thing we have to proclaim to the world, to proclaim to everybody, is that the Spirit indeed dwells in our hearts. By turning to it with full attention, we too can live out the fullness of love. We too can live out the power that is the Kingdom of God. Part of the discipline of mediation is that it teaches us to stay in that love, come what may.' (John Main 'The Way of Love.)

Through many tragic circumstances in my life, I had been to the jumping-off point when I lost my all, my reason for living and hoping. Upon recovering from my sadness and madness, I discovered in my new adulthood things about myself and my family, my then value system that was all myth. I discovered that the mantra I lived by, the code of ethics I subscribed to, and the 'story' I had told myself since childhood to get by and survive, to a great degree were not true. In fact, I had been, to a large degree, living a myth, without recognising it as such. The human truth of the Jesus I was taught to believe as a child varied greatly from the Jesus that now evolves within.

When the historical Jesus becomes someone who can inspire us and teach us about life outside Christian myth; then this involves, and perhaps is the consequence of the act of forgiving Jesus for being human. It is part of his fate, to be one of the greatest myths of human history. But this does not erase the voiceprint of a historical figure. True, it makes Jesus an enigma, but it does not eliminate the basic fact of his humanity. So on the scales of belief, my own and by further investigation, like an anthropologist digging up some unidentified bones and trying to make some sense of the find, I endorse it. Not so much from a historical aspect but from agreement of factual verification of believers.

I returned to journal down some beliefs that have evolved over the centuries in support of what may be compared to what Winston Churchill stated about Russia at the end of WW11- 'It is a riddle, wrapped in a mystery, inside an enigma.' Mine is more an endorsement of the existence of Christ breaking the riddle, unwrapping the mystery, which leans to fact more than fiction or enigma. God throughout the Bible spoke through the prophets to prove he was God. He foretold the future, taught them to verify who he was, to prove to people that those who spoke were true prophets, and to draw mankind to worship him only. The 100% accuracy of the prophecies that can be uncovered in the Bible that came true is proof of the existence of God and of Jesus if one opens the mind to these documented proofs.

'I am God, and there is none like me. Declaring the end from the beginning, and from ancient times the things that are not yet done saying, 'My counsel shall stand, and I will do all my pleasure:' (Isaiah 46: 10-11). There are many hundreds of perditions that have come true from the time of Christ, 30 AD until today. Perhaps the most pertinent right now are those that relate to Russia and the nations of Islam. Predicted ca. 10th Century BC: Psalm 120:5-7 predicted that Russians and Arabia would be people that hate peace and embrace War. Fulfilled in 600 AD to the present for Arabia: when the Arabian prophet Muhammad spread his new religion of Islam, he used wars to do it and his followers have been warring ever since. Russia is still warring today but the ultimate war will come in the future as prophesied in Ezekiel 38-39, when they will lead a group of nations to fight Israel. It is to be hoped that the request of Our Lady of Fatima to pray for the conversation of Russia in this 21st Century will stave off this biblical prophecy.

The Bible states a reference to the time Jesus was put on the cross which is confirmed here: 'Now from the sixth hour there was darkness over all the land until the ninth hour.' The sixth hour is noon and the ninth hour, is 3 P.M. Thus we see that the historian Thallus was trying to explain the odd occurrence of the sky being dark at noon when the crucifixion of Jesus was an eclipse. Africanus also quoted Pythagoras a Greek historian who lived in the 2nd century AD and also wrote of the eclipse occurring on the day Jesus was crucified. This again confirms non-Christian sources that confirm the account of Jesus being a real person who lived as well as confirms the account of his crucifixion straight from the bible. And another bible quote: 'at the death of Christ, the sun darkened, the earth trembled and the dead arose and appeared too many.'

 Lucian (Born 115AD) was a well-known Greek satirist and a travelling lecturer. More than eighty works bear his name. He mocked Christians in his writing, but at the same time provided evidence that Jesus was real. 'He was second only to that one whom they worship today, the man in Palestine who was crucified because he brought this new form of initiation into the world.' He goes on to describe the beliefs of Christians, the personal sacrifices they make, and their transgression from denying Greek Gods to worship of this

Christian God. And being all on one level with this God in their belief for eternity. Lucian does not mention Christ by name but he confirms his existence that he was crucified in 'Palestine', had followers who believed in eternal life and that they were equal to Jesus Christ.

Lucian even mentions that Christians deny all other gods and believe in 'faith alone.' This again is in accordance with the Bible's clear statements about the Christian faith and provides more evidence of the existence of Christ, that 'the man in Palestine, did really exist.' Gaius Suetonius Tranquillus, known as Suetonius (ca.69/75)- was a Roman historian belonging to the equestrian order era in the early Imperial era. His most important surviving work is a set of biographies of twelve successive Roman rulers from Julius Caesar to Domitian, entitled 'De Vita Caesium'.

In the apparent description of his writing, he states- 'The Emperor Claudius reigned 41AD to 524 AD.' Suetonius reports his dealings with the eastern Roman Empire, that is, with Greece and Macedonia, and with Lycian, Rhodesians, and Trojans. He then reports that the Emperor expelled Jews from Rome since they 'constantly made disturbances at the instigation of Christ.' Sceptics will point to the different spelling to say that's not the Jesus he's talking about. But again, with the totality of evidence, it's obvious that followers of Jesus in the Roman Empire were persecuted by Roman authorities. It certainly falls in line with other chronicles and biblical historical parchments that the Romans who followed Jesus were being punished for it. And it holds with the Roman record that has survived in time which clearly shows "We have to stamp out these followers of Jesus" after his death and resurrection.

There is a great logical fallacy among Bible sceptics, atheists and those who challenge Christianity that says, when discussing historical aspects of the Bible 'you can't use the Bible as proof that Jesus existed. You use non- Bible sources!' To which this author says

' Well, why not?' The four Gospels of the Bible are bibliographical accounts of the life of Jesus. The normal objective measure of the reliability of historical documents is 1.) the number of available copies of ancient manuscripts. 2.) The time span between original versions and the date of those copies is still in existence today. When examined under this standard, the Bible proves to provide a treasure trove of proof and evidence that Jesus really existed. All other non-biblical historical evidence supports and reinforces this. Manuscript fragments of the New Testament documents, written between 50-100 AD, support all the biblical and non-biblical evidence of the existence of Jesus Christ.

CHAPTER 5.

THE LOVE OF THE ONE

The record of the life, ministry, death and resurrection of Jesus Christ has more evidence and proof than any other person from antiquity. Jesus believed that he was just a regular man but he was reportedly the son of God, who gave his life on the cross that so many historians knew about, to take the punishment for the wrongdoings of humanity. It takes faith and trust in that sacrifice to receive him. Jesus said: 'Behold, I stand at the door, and knock: if any man hears my voice, and opens the door, I will come into him and will sup with him, and he with me. To him that overcomes will I grant to sit with me in my throne, even as I also overcame and I sit down with my Father in his throne.'- 11 Revelation 3: 20-21.

Jesus obviously wants us to believe in him based on volumes of documented evidence of his birth, death, resurrection, ascension into heaven. If we are to be free from our defects of character, we have to be committed to our lives here and now to have eternal life in the hereafter and reign with him. So now that it is established that He existed, what is it that he is really asking of us? I began to ponder this thought. Still determined to further delve into the matter of faith now and not the evidence of his existence. Did I really need to do that though? What is it that this God of my inner spirit is asking of me? I was thinking. Jesus in the scriptures particularly the Sermon on the Mount, in Matthew's gospel points out the essence of his teaching: Jesus is consistently seen to be merciful, gracious, faithful, forgiving, and steadfast in love. Of course, it is not always easy on a daily basis, to live by this Credo. But if Jesus is the image of his Father i.e. the Universal God figure that is nonetheless hard to believe in his existence in the void, and we are called to imitate him -then it stands to reason that the way to live by these principles is to bring those five adjectives into play. So practicing mindfulness as Christ dictated in his Sermon on the Mount is to appreciate the need for his grace- that gift that can only be absorbed by doing unto others as they would have us do unto you. Those five adjectives of mercy, grace, faith, forgiveness and steadfastness seem to be the catalysts of human action for the betterment of oneself and our fellow man. If that's all there is to it, then it's worth a shot to try this Christ credo for a better life- being a believer or a nonbeliever.

Jesus was only on earth as a man for a short time. He was visited by shepherds as a witness to his coming for they had been told already by an angel of his birth. Likewise, Magi Kings had followed a star from the east to the place of his birth; offering gifts of gold, frankincense and myrrh. Apart from his preaching to the priests of the temple at age 12, he goes missing for 18 years and next appears when he returns from 40-day fasting in the desert and is baptised by John the Baptist in the river Jordan.

He preached for the next three years to his followers performed many miracles, predicted future events, and ultimately sacrificed himself on the cross for the wrongdoings of mankind, died and was buried at age 33, rose again from the dead three days later, visited his followers and ascended into the heavens. Jesus not only fulfilled his own spoken prophecy in his lifetime, he predicted events that were to come to pass sometime in the future. One of the ministries was that of a prophet. Jesus had predicted that 'heaven and earth will pass away, but my words will not pass away' (Mathew 24:35)-to date his words still echo throughout Christendom, read and believed by untold millions. Mary of Bethany poured oil on the body of Jesus in her anticipation of his death. She was rebuked by the disciples for wasting the oil. Jesus chastised them saying that her story would be retold wherever the gospel was preached. This has always come to pass.

Jesus also predicted that one of his own would betray him. This was literally fulfilled by Judas. Jesus predicted that Peter would deny him three times before the cock crowed. This too came to pass. He predicted that he would suffer at the hands of religious rulers. On the night he was arrested the religious rulers allowed him to be beaten. Jesus predicted he would die in Jerusalem and upon the cross. Both predictions took place. He predicted that he would die during the Passover and would rise again in three days. This is well documented as having occurred as he predicted.

Many other events such as the destruction of the City of Jerusalem within one generation, the destruction of the Temple, the scattering of the Jewish people from their land, their captivity and the ruling of the Holy Land by the Gentiles, the persecution of the Jewish people and though persecuted, the nation of Jews would survive-all of these predictions have been literally fulfilled. These facts demonstrate beyond any doubt that Jesus was indeed a genuine prophet. During his earthly ministry, Jesus touched and transformed countless lives. Like other events in the life of Jesus, all his miracles were documented by eyewitnesses. The Gospels record 37 of these and are mentioned in various texts by the four writers Mathew, Mark, Luke and John. The ability at age 12 to interpret holy scriptures and teach wise scribes and priests in the Temple of Jerusalem would seem like a miracle to them at the time for one with apparently limited formal education other than biblical instruction of the Torah which all Jewish boys were taught as children.

He went on to perform many miracles over the remaining 3 years of his remaining time on earth before he was crucified. This was followed by healing the sick, casting out evil spirits from the possessed, cleansing those diseased; restoring the use of limbs, restoring the sight of the blind and hearing of the deaf; calming the sea, ensuring a major fish catch, feeding the multitude, walking on water, bringing people back to life and many more.

It is not so difficult in this modern age to add fact with myth to justify the miracles of Christ whilst on earth. In point of fact, I shall use as examples here two ' miracles' in the modern age which will add credence to the fact that Christ did perform miracles whilst on earth as defined biblically and verified by historical records.

Nikola Tesla was born in 1856 in Croatia, then part of the Austro-Hungarian Empire. His father was a priest in the Serbian Orthodox church and his mother managed the family's farm. In 1863 Tesla's brother Daniel was killed in a riding accident. The shock of the loss unsettled the 7-year-old Tesla, who reported seeing visions—the first signs of his lifelong mental illnesses. Still, as a child, whilst out walking by a river on a fishing trip with his uncle he demonstrated how to catch fish in large quantities. He simply placed his hands in the river and it seemed by a miraculous intervention a large quantity of dead fish rose to the surface of the river as he had predicted.

In his early twenties, Tesla studied math and physics at the Technical University of Graz and philosophy at the University of Prague. In 1882, while on a walk, he came up with the idea for a brushless AC motor, making the first sketches of its rotating electromagnets in the sand of the path. Later that year he moved to Paris and got a job repairing direct current (DC) power plants with the Continental Edison Company. Two years later he immigrated to the United States. Tesla arrived in New York in 1884 and was hired as an engineer at Thomas Edison's Manhattan headquarters. He worked there for a year, impressing Edison with his diligence and ingenuity. At one point Edison told Tesla he would pay $50,000 for an improved design for his DC dynamos. After months of experimentation, Tesla presented a solution and asked for the money. Edison demurred, saying, "Tesla, you don't understand our American humour." Tesla quit soon after. In 1887 and 1888 he was granted more than 30 **patents for his inventions and invited to address the American**

Institute of Electrical Engineers on his work. His lecture caught the attention of George Westinghouse, the inventor who had launched the first AC power system near Boston and was Edison's major competitor in the "Battle of the Currents." Westinghouse hired Tesla, licensed the patents for his AC motor and gave him his own lab. Buoyed by Westinghouse's royalties, Tesla struck out on his own again. But Westinghouse was soon forced by his backers to renegotiate their contract, with Tesla relinquishing his royalty rights. In the 1890s Tesla invented electric oscillators, meters, improved lights and the high-voltage transformer known as the Tesla coil. He also experimented with X-rays, gave short-range demonstrations of radio communication two years before Guglielmo Marconi and piloted a radio-controlled boat around a pool in Madison Square Garden. Together, Tesla and Westinghouse lit and partnered with General Electric to install AC generators at Niagara Falls, creating the first modern power station.

In 1895 Tesla's New York lab burned, destroying years' worth of notes and equipment. Tesla relocated to Colorado Springs for two years, returning to New York in 1900. He secured backing from financiers and built a global communications network centred on a giant tower at Wardenclyffe, on Long Island. But funds ran out and Morgan balked at Tesla's grandiose schemes. During this period he successfully created an electric coil that created a thunderstorm and lightning in the sky but its power generated too much heat and burnt out the main electricity supply blacking out the city of Colorado Springs electricity supply and main generator that only Tesla was able to fix. He invented the forerunner tower to wifi and had a vision for a worldwide mobile network. Tesla lived his last decades in a New York hotel, working on new inventions even as his energy and mental health faded. His obsession with the number three and fastidious washing were dismissed as the eccentricities of genius. He spent his final years feeding—and, he claimed, communicating with the city's pigeons.

After the bombing of Pearl Harbour by the Japanese, Tesla contacted the US military with a solution to melt the motors of aircraft with a death ray invention he had plans for. It would destroy the aircraft motors as far away as 200 miles in the event of further attacks. Tesla died in his room on January 7, 1943, soon after advising the military of his plan. The morning after his death his trunk full of futuristic plans and designs were collected by US government officials and were not available for release until twenty years after his death. Many of the marvels of modern science and technology have since been built based on his plans. Later in 1943, the U.S. Supreme Court voided four of Marconi's key patents, belatedly acknowledging Tesla's innovations in radio. The AC system he championed and improved remains the global standard for power transmission to this very day. He knew how to harness energy from the universe's source and his belief was that a higher power guided his efforts.

Harry Houdini/, born; March 24, 1874 – October 31, 1926) was an American escape artist, illusionist and stuntman, noted for his escape acts. He first attracted notice in vaudeville in the United States and then as "Harry Handcuff Houdini" on a tour of Europe, where he challenged police forces to keep him locked up. Soon he extended his repertoire to include chains, ropes slung from skyscrapers, straight jackets under water, and having to escape from and hold his breath inside a sealed milk can with water in it. In 1904, thousands watched as he tried to escape from special handcuffs commissioned by London's Daily Mirror, keeping them in suspense for an hour. Another stunt saw him buried alive and only just able to claw himself to the surface, emerging in a state of near-breakdown. While many suspected that these escapes were faked, Houdini presented himself as the scourge of fake spiritualists. As President of the Society of American Magicians, he was keen to uphold professional standards and expose fraudulent artists. He was also quick to sue anyone who imitated his escape stunts. From 1907 and throughout the 1910s, Houdini performed with great success in the United States.

He freed himself from jails, handcuffs, chains, ropes, and straight jackets, often while hanging from a rope in sight of street audiences. Because of imitators, Houdini put his "handcuff act" behind him on January 25, 1908, and began escaping from a locked, water-filled milk can. The possibility of failure and death thrilled his audiences. Houdini also expanded his repertoire with his escape challenge act, in which he invited the public to devise contraptions to hold him. These included nailed packing crates (sometimes lowered into water), riveted boilers, wet sheets, mail bags, and even the belly of a whale that had washed ashore in Boston. Brewers in Scranton, Pennsylvania, and other cities challenged Houdini to escape from a barrel after they filled it with beer.
There is no supporting evidence for it ever having happened, such as a newspaper account, and Houdini tended to change the location and details as if to misdirect. The location most often cited is the Belle Isle Bridge in Detroit on November 27, 1906. But newspaper accounts of Houdini's bridge jump that day make no mention of a frozen river. People gathered to see the 'Handcuff King', the great Harry Houdini himself be nailed in a box and thrown into a cold, dirty river. Sometimes the crowd would grow to such a colossal size that the police had to interfere and drive Houdini away in the boat with his beloved box.

Recently I discovered a story in Houdini's own words in a biographical article from Hearty's in 1919 called ' Nearly Dying for a Living. Here the location is Pittsburgh and, interestingly, he does mention being lowered in his locked box through a hole in the ice. "I lay flat on my back, tight up against the ice, and breathed. Then I found that the water came in little intermittent waves and that by keeping my face close against the ice I could move about and get an occasional breath. I still held in my hands the handcuffs that I had removed from my wrists, and with these pressed against the ice I began a circular movement. And suddenly I bobbed up through the hole, and the men reached down and lifted me out onto the ice, wrapped me up and hurried me to my hotel. The crowd that had come to see me and my assistants believed that I had been drowned and, although I didn't hear it, they say that a mighty cheer went up when I appeared.

One point of interest is that Houdini says he couldn't hear the cheers of the crowd when he surfaced. This strikes me as a very believable detail that you wouldn't find in a purely fictionalised account.. It is possible Houdini is saved from his ice-bound grave by the spirit of his dead mother. When he hears her voice calls out to him and leads him to the hole in the ice. Maybe it was divine intervention that saved Houdini from a power greater than himself. After Houdini was shacked and nailed into a heavy packing crate. The crate would be wound in ropes and weighed down with steel weights. It would then be sent down a plank or lowered via block and tackled into the water. In a few minutes, Houdini would come to the surface free. The box would be retrieved and found to still be sealed.

Now what has this got to do with Christ's time on earth and the miracles that are associated with him? Well nothing really, except to say that in Tesla's case, he harnessed the power of the universe's energy and invented many things and displayed the power of light over darkness, and over control of the weather by creating a thunderstorm and causing lightning to strike were he said it would. Tesla was a realist with a vision to the future whose vision and plans mankind benefits from to this very day. Houdini on the other hand was an illusionist who dealt with magic trickery to achieve his acts of danger and intrigue for entertainment purposes. He proved that the power of myth can easily be mistaken for reality by his acts. In point of fact, his underwater escapades ultimately killed him, as he drowned in a tank whilst performing.

* * * * * * *

Jesus, to the people of his time, may have seen in him both a Tesla of miraculous deeds and a Houdini of illusion in some of the miracles he performed. Ultimately the greatest of his acts was to sacrifice himself for the defects of the character of mankind in order that we all may be forgiven and saved in spite of our wrongdoing. The spirit of the man defies earthly reason, for who else of God-like disposition in the history of the world has sacrificed himself for humanity, dying on the cross, rising from the dead three days later, and in a transition state visits his disciples, performs further miracles then ascends, body and soul into the heavens with some of his followers swearing testimony to this happening.

It has been considered by modern-day writings, possibly totally mythical, that Augustus, the then Roman leader Caesar Augustus, after the murder of his foster father Julius Caesar, had scribes record the myth of himself being 'Messiah.' He manufactured the story, having Saul, a Roman soldier, go forth and recruit followers after his so-called 'conversion' on the road to Damascus. If one were to believe such a 'story' this may have occurred before Christ's ascension into heaven. However, the Bible in Acts, clearly indicates Saul's (St.Paul's) conversion occurred well after the Ascension. It is a moot point and really is essentially trivia: a case of the story of Christ on earth can not be proven or disproven, much less the case for Caesar Augustus being the true Messiah!

CHAPTER 6.

TESTIMONY OF THE ONE

There is more documented evidence, in the Bible and other credible recorded literature that confirms the reality of the Christ on earth story. Myth or reality, modern-day man is either a believer or a disbeliever. I have my doubts in my logical linear half-brain-about a living Christ on earth but documented evidence from many sources had me to reconsider. A living Christ is an inward thing, I have me to accept this as a belief. Be it Christ in the manifest of Roman times, Christ in the biblical account that pacifies the brain of traditional believers or a Christ of one's own imagination is not the concern. The dead Christ can only, to my mind, be a Christ of the imagination, of an inner consciousness- a manifestation, whatever realm one chooses to follow.

It is not my task here to throw out the baby with the bathwater, but merely do my best to grow an embryonic manifestation of the Christ spirit for myself and give you, dear reader, words to consider on this subject. My writings here foretold occurred well after my return to Australia from my third Camino. My mind of The Way was a healing mind, an enquiring mind and a mind of a sceptic to believe in something other than what the world I grew up in had to offer and indeed the current material world, other than a ' 'Santiago Traveling wanderer ' has to offer. So the text surrounding the signs of the zodiacs, the parallels relating to past spiritual leaders, doctrinaires of faith and morals, the signs and symbols in the planets, in the end, count, for little more than a puff of smoke in the reality of the now. I guess I begin to see what Christ reportedly said 'The kingdom of heaven is within.' When one analyses by deconstructing the Christ of miracle, mystery and authority, it is a short step to wondering if the whole story of Christ is a myth. Thinking on that premise, and the deepest construct of a creative human spirituality, the historical Jesus, as such, never existed. However, very few history and biblical studies draw the conclusion that a Jesus of the old story never existed. The main division in scholastic concerns is how to appropriate Jesus.

Was he an apocalyptic or avatar? Few researchers question if he ever lived. Still, on a popular level, Jesus, understood as a myth, and strictly a myth, seems to be gaining ground. So, was he or wasn't he? Did he ever live or is it all just a good story? Critical examination of Christian gospels, especially with the rise of formal criticism, does recommend the conclusion that Jesus as the centre of Christian dogma emerged in the itinerant preaching of the earliest Jesus movement.

Basically, people spoke in the manner of the 'living' Jesus who had died. Preachers spoke 'in the spirit of Jesus,' thus making him alive in their witness. The Gospel of John is historical in the sense that it records the 'speaking in the spirit of Jesus.' This was the charisma of the early Church which, of course, eventually needed to be regulated in some form. The earliest social movements related to Jesus preserved his memory in this way. The parables and aphorisms of Jesus are a case in point. The forms of speech of this 'historic' Jesus, a base mode of teaching, were preserved, if re-interpreted, in the teaching and preaching of the next generation. Formal criticism was all about finding the voiceprint of the teacher that was carried forward in new shapes, by students

of this form. Now comes the myth. It all starts by asking how much of the Jesus material is fictional, arising from later generations who spoke 'In the name of Jesus' without actually saying anything the historical Jesus said. Also, how much of the Jesus material can be identified with confidence as an originating voice point, something close to historical?

The line between these two questions is often blurry, and it is exactly this blurriness that inspires the possibility that all the material is mythical, that is, all the material is made up 'in the name of Jesus.' Once that step is taken, the natural conclusion is that there is no historical Jesus. It is actually hard to prove there was a historical Jesus using conventional forms of history. Jesus was unknown. We have to remember that the big name of his lifetime was Socrates. Everybody, including Jesus, had heard of Socrates. He was famous. Jesus, as a Galilean of his time was not famous and had no chance as his birthright of ever being famous. In light of the rise of Christianity, it is hard to imagine that Jesus was an unknown.

He may have been illiterate and poor as was his community. No one was able to hire scribes to read great works to them, record great thoughts or send letters home. Still, he was a carpenter's son so he would have perhaps understood mathematics and his reported knowledge of preaching to the scribes in the temple proves otherwise. The Christian gospels record the popularity of Jesus and his large following is almost certainly imaginary. His crucifixion by the Roman authorities was done without blinking nobody in a long line of nobody rabble-rousers. We look at Jesus from the perspective of 2000 years of history, and he seems to us to be among the greats. Indeed, he is amongst the greats, but an immediate experience of his life belongs to a minor school or movement that was largely ignored and mostly unknown. Accordingly, it is not possible to expect a great recovery of contemporary witness to his life and times.

What we can expect is second and third- and third-generation historians mentioning him in light of a new and rising movement that claims him as the true Caesar (the Lord, Saviour, and the Son of God). Ancient historians and those not ancient question: Who was this Jesus and who were his people? Later historians know about the rising movement and relay whatever information they can gather regarding its founder. The information is humble. It concerns the followers who called him 'The Christ.' His relationship to another teacher named John the Baptist, that he was crucified, that his followers are poor and ignorant. That there were lies and rumours spread about him. This is what we can read in Josephus, Tacitus, Suetonius, the letter of Pliny the Younger and others - Mar-ben Saparion, Lucian and Samosata to name but a few of the many. So why then does the idea that Jesus never was persist and gain popular assent?   The answer is the plain fact that despite the aforementioned, there is contemporary witness to the Jesus of history. The earliest we can get is Paul, an educated Roman soldier, who said that Jesus was once historical (2 Cor 5:16)and met and knew 'the brother of the Lord.' (Gal 1:19).

Still, it remains simply true that there has never been an eyewitness report about any incident in the life of Christ. This simple fact is often the foundation for believing Jesus was only purely a myth.

The second element that supports the belief Jesus was a myth emerges because this belief is partially correct. Much about Jesus is indeed a myth. Really, much about anybody, including our own self is mythical. With Jesus, like with Confucius or other ancient teachers about whom nothing really exists, myth comes with the package. The earliest Christian movement did interpret Jesus in the light of Jewish scripture; especially the prophets. The dying and rising of Jesus is consistent with the notion of divine individuation in pagan Gods, a biblical reference to the notion of regeneration is prevalent. Jesus, his death and resurrection, fits right in with these common, and universal, mythical patterns. Early educated Christians could draw upon both Jewish, Greek and later Roman sources in this regard. Thirdly, it is a plain fact that many early Christian preachers spoke in the name of Jesus, saying things that Jesus never said. Christianity created a cache of Jesus sayings that contained both historical and non-historical inspired sayings about the nature of Jesus, his divinity and the realm of the Kingdom of God. Whilst the commentary on the parables is made up the use of parables is not. Jesus never said 'I and the Father are one.' (John 10:30) but rather he used a parable like 'a sower went out to sow his seed.' (Mark 4:3). and Mark interpreted the sower parable as an allegory about the quality of Christian believers. So, even within the Christian sources that witness Jesus, much of the witness is myth.

There is not much any historian can do about this situation except to understand it. Still, it does not prove the case that Jesus never existed. We all want something to believe, and sometimes when we used to feel certain about becoming questionable, the reaction is to throw the whole thing out. I guess I felt this way in the year my whole world seemed to come unhinged. I believed many things about my life from childhood to adulthood that turned out to be a myth.

But in the now reality of the late afternoon of my life, I lean more to the spirit of the Christ consciousness and guidance as such as a step to the inner kingdom; a spirit of mindfulness of a Jesus of the manifest that guides me. In this, I need to quiet my mind to logical thought processes and listen to the inner voice of reason to guide my steps. Lead kindly light, lead through me on.

Now one may lean on the miracles of Christ on earth to justify the message of his existence and the purpose of his mission. Still, I drew more hope on the miracles that transpired after his death, for they are more relevant to me in this time of my manifested belief in the risen Christ. So it is to him I turn now, overlooking the myth of it all and focusing on his word, his deeds and the meaning of these stories since told after his resurrection, before his ascension into the heavens.

It is on Christ I now call in this moment of mediation, to have him guide my fingers to write now what he dictates to me as guidance to imitate what it is he is now asking. Jesus often walked by the Sea of Galilee observing the fishermen as they rowed their boats, cast their nets and hauled in the catch. He would note how they worked diligently to drag the nest in when fish were plentiful. It was on those occasions that He made a mental note, not only of their physical strength and capability but their demure; their temperament under pressure of completing the task before the tide changed, who showed leadership qualities, who followed the leader, who got angry, who laughed the most when things went wrong. For all his visits he began to create a profile in his head of who he wanted to recruit for the task ahead, when he would go forth to teach and preach his message of salvation. He would carefully choose the best twelve to encourage them to leave their boats and follow him to become ' fishers of men.' They were such a rough and ready lot but he could see into their hearts honest m of faith, courage, determination and great forth rightfulness.

Jesus gained the confidence of these fishermen over the many visits he made to the Sea of Galilee where he may well have eaten carp and the Tilapia, which later became known as 'St. Peter's fish,' These are the fish which stipulates the region and are often eaten throughout the Israel Holy Land. It was there that the local fishermen reportedly listened with amazement to his teachings of the kingdom and He groomed many to the kingdom of heaven. They had possibly heard of the marvel of his turning water into wine (John 2:1-12) at the marriage feast of Cana, and reports of His curing the blind and casting out demons from the possessed men, or some may have been present when he healed the Nobleman's son (John 4:46-54) or raised Lazarets from the dead.

On an appointed day Jesus had concluded that he needed time out to choose those most worthy of teaching the message of redemption from sin, and the power of living in this world but not of it, being always mindful of the 'Holy Spirit, the third person of the Trinity ' which would come about by His sacrifice of death for mankind and ultimate resurrection and ascension into heaven. Jesus went up to a mountainside and called to him those he wanted, and they came to him. He appointed twelve that they might be with him and that he might send them out to preach and to have authority to drive out demons. These are the twelve he appointed: Simon (to whom he gave the name Peter), James son of Zebedee and his brother John (to them he gave the name Boanerges, which means "sons of thunder"), Andrew, Philip, Bartholomew, Matthew, Thomas, James son of Alphaeus, Thaddaeus, Simon the Zealot and Judas Iscariot, who eventually betrayed him. He had taught them to lay down their net and became fishers of men, and in their travels far and wide throughout the land they saw him perform even more miracles, like the feeding of the 5000 who attended his sermon on the mount.

The apostles could only find five loaves and three fish from the attendees they asked to feed the people. When they had told Jesus of this, he commanded that they break the bread into small pieces and the fish likewise and begin to feed the crowd. To the amazement of all the crowd was fed and when they collected the leftovers they gathered twelve baskets. This account of the miracle has been recorded in the Gospels of Evangelists Matthew, Mark, Luke and John and stands as a testament of truth to this very day. Jesus called his twelve disciples to him and gave them authority to drive out impure spirits and to heal every disease and sickness. These are the names of the twelve apostles: first, Simon (who is called Peter) and his brother Andrew; James son of Zebedee, and his brother John; Philip and Bartholomew; Thomas and Matthew the tax collector; James Son of Alhpaeus, and Thaddaeus; Simon the Zealot and Judas Iscariot, who betrayed him. Is it significant that Christ chose Twelve apostles? Yes, it was so because Jesus chose the Twelve as they represent the Twelve Tribes of Israel, thus showing a link between the Old Covenant and the New Covenant.

The German theologian Friedrich Justus Knecht (d. 1921) reflects on the question, "Why'd our Lord Jesus Christ choose for this stupendous office twelve ignorant men, of a low station in life, and of no importance in the eyes of the world?" He answers, "It wIt to show to the whole world that the maintenance and spread of the Church and her doctrine were not due to human wisdom and learning, but solely to His grace and protection. 'The foolish things of the world hath God chosen that He may confound the wise, and the weak things of the world hath God chosen that He may confound the strong; and the base things of the world, and the things that are contemptible, hath God chosen; and things that are not, that He might bring to naught things that are: that no flesh should glory in His sight' (i Cor. i, 27. 28. 29)."

St. Jerome comments on this passage saying, "A kind and merciful Lord and Master does not envy His servants and disciples a share in His powers. As Himself had cured every sickness and disease, He imparted the same power to His Apostles. But there is a wide difference between having and imparting, between giving and receiving. Whatever He does He does with the power of a master, whatever they do it is with confession of their own weakness, as they speak, In the name of Jesus rise and walk. (Acts 3:6.)

A catalogue of the names of the Apostles is given so that all false Apostles might be excluded. The names of the twelve Apostles are these; First, Simon who is called Peter, and Andrew his brother. To arrange them in order according to their merit is His alone who searches the secrets of all hearts. But Simon is placed first, having the surname of Peter given to distinguish him from the other Simon surnamed Chananæus, from the village of Chana in Galilee where the Lord turned the water into wine." But it is not the miracles whilst he was on earth that the t Apostles ultimately retold to the followers of Jesus, but those they told after his death on the cross, resurrection and ascension into heaven.

Firstly, let us recall when Jesus advised them at the Last Supper of the sacrifice he was to make the next day. He had broken the bread and raised his glass of wine in a farewell toast with a deep and meaningful message:" Take an eat of this unleavened bread, for this is the body, and drink of this wine, for this is my blood. When you eat this bread and drink this wine, do this in commemoration of me." This is the very same sacrifice of the body and blood of Christ that is carried out throughout Christendom to this very day. The last of the miracles performed by Christ was reported by the apostles and the Roman guards who came to the garden of Gethsemane to take Jesus away to be executed. Apparently when the Romans arrived to capture Jesus, the apostle Peter picked up a sword and cut off the ear of Manchus, the leader of the Roman guard. Jesus unperturbed picked up the ear and reattached it—unbloodied, unscathed, and as good as new. Manchus must have felt both bewilderment and amazement that his sworn enemy could show him such kindness. This was Jesus' last miracle before his death, and maybe the one that is most significant for us.

It was significant that Jesus was calm, cool and collected at this time, as he had already resolved himself to his appointed hour to be crucified.

We know from the biblical text of Matthew, Mark, Luke and John and historical reports that Jesus was betrayed by Judas Iscariot, one of the twelve chosen ones, who was paid thirty pieces of silver by the authorities for this act and ultimately hung himself in shame and remorse when the guilt crime of blasphemy was sentenced on Jesus and he was led away to be crucified.   We know of Peter's denial that he did not know Christ and was not his follower. He too suffered much for his fearful defect at the time. After the crucifixion, the apostles retreated to a meeting room in fear for their lives. They knew that the Romans and Pharisees would be on the lookout for Jesus' apostles and disciples. The Roman authority in particular sought to quell any chance of a religious revival being formed after the death, and the report of His being raised from the dead.

So all the apostles with the exception of Thomas were gathered in that upper room, possibly where the last supper had been held on the previous Thursday evening. They were there out of fear of being captured and persecuted by The Roman authority and were lost as to what they should do next, and considered the best thing to do was go back to the Sea of Galilee and return to their occupation as fishermen. It was for a brief encounter that Jesus appeared to them and counselled them not to be afraid and to carry out their duties as he had instructed them to do.

CHAPTER 7.

IN CHRIST'S REFORMATION

It was then, as stated in the Gnostic gospel, that Mary Magdalene appeared as a disciple, surprising them with news that she had spoken to the Lord who had risen from the tomb. For Jesus had singled her out for special teachings. Jesus said to her, "Do not cling to me, because I have not yet ascended to...my Father and your Father, to my God and your God." So Mary of Magdala went and told the disciples that she had seen the Lord and that he had said these things to her. Mary is the only one other than the apostles to be mentioned by name who abodes in the upper room. (Acts 1:12–26) In this excerpt, the other disciples are discouraged and grieving Jesus' death. Mary stands up and attempts to comfort them, reminding them that Jesus' presence remained with them. For he had been brought from an empty tomb, a Risen Saviour with victory over sin and death. On this day, a new order of existence was born. Jesus was resurrected from the dead! Nothing like this had ever happened before. Resurrection is not resuscitation, like the people Jesus brought back to life—they died again. Resurrection is not reincarnation. Resurrection is not a mystical vision or a phantom appearance by a ghost. Resurrection is the remaking, the transforming of matter in this created order. It becomes something new, something that has never before existed. The Apostles so deeply desired the accompaniment of Mary as they waited in the Upper Room. Mary, filled with the Spirit, had a quiet attraction that drew them, interiorly, closer to God. They gathered around her for strength and insight as they pondered the full impact of Jesus' resurrection.

Thomas was not present at the time when the Apostles and Mary Magdalene told him of Jesus' appearance, so they gathered once more in the Upper room in the hope of his return visit. Thomas had a self-imposed criterion for believing in Jesus' resurrection, stating, "Unless I see and unless I can touch the evidence, I will never believe" (John 20:25). Thomas actually wanted not only to see Jesus, he wanted to touch Jesus intimately, putting his finger in the nail holes and his hand into the side of Jesus: not just as proof, I think, but also a way to reconnect with the Jesus who died and has now returned. Then Jesus appeared to them, again filled their hearts with the power of the Holy Spirit, and tongues of fire danced over their heads like candle flames. Thomas was still not convinced, seeing this as perhaps an imaginary collective wishful vision of all. Jesus then offered Thomas his side saying; " Place your fingers here and feel the wound in my side, and see and touch the wounds on my wrist." Thomas fell to his knees in adoration saying; " My Lord and my God." Jesus reportedly stated; " Thomas, because thou hast seen me, thou hast believed: blessed are they that have not seen, and yet still believe."   So it was there in that Upper room the apostles meditated on the Risen Christ and tongues of fire appeared above their heads and they were filled with the Holy Spirit.

The Bible records at least eight appearances of the resurrected Jesus to different people at various times and locations over a 40-day period before He ascended into heaven. In each of these appearances, there is a victory. First, Jesus appeared to Mary Magdalene at the tomb (Mark 16:9). Mary was weeping at the tomb, thinking she had lost Jesus forever. Jesus appeared and brought victory over despair. Second, Jesus appeared to other women as they were leaving the tomb (Matthew 28:9-10). They thought he was dead, but he appeared to them, and they worshipped Him, bringing victory over death.

Third, Jesus met up with two disciples on the road to Emmaus (Luke 24:13-32). These men were talking about all the week's events surrounding Jesus. They didn't understand what had happened. Jesus talked with them and stayed with them until they understood. Jesus brought victory over confusion.

Fourth, Jesus appeared to 10 disciples who were hiding together (Luke 24:36-43; John 20:19-25). These disciples were afraid of what might happen to them since Jesus had been killed. Jesus brought victory over fear.

Fifth, Jesus appeared to all remaining disciples (Mark 16:14; John 20:26-31). Thomas, who had doubted Jesus' resurrection, was with them this time. Jesus brought victory over doubt.

Sixth, Jesus appeared to seven disciples, including Peter, who had denied Jesus three times (John 21). At this appearance, Jesus puts Peter back into ministry. Jesus brought victory over failure.

Seventh, Jesus appeared to the 11 disciples at a pre-arranged location on a mountain in Galilee (Matthew 28:16-20). There Jesus told them He had been given all power and authority. He gave His followers the great commission to make disciples. Jesus brought victory over any other power.

Eighth, Jesus finally appeared to as many as 500 of His followers at one time. He confirmed the completion of His mission and the promise of the Holy Spirit (Luke 22:44-49; Acts 1:3-8). Jesus had victory over all things. The remaining apostles, knowing their master's intention for them to be ' Fishers of men,' returned to the boats to catch fish, for they were uncertain of hope to 'Let go and let God,' in taking the next step to preach the message of Jesus. It was whilst they were fishing on one occasion that Jesus appeared to them walking on the waters off the Sea of Galilee. Jesus beckoned Peter to come to him and not be afraid to walk upon the water. Peter gained enough confidence to trust the Master and began to walk upon the water, but fear entered his heart and he began to sink, fearing he might drown, he reached up and clung to the boat returning to its safety. Jesus appeared in the boat no doubt warning them of lacking faith in his mission for them. (John 6:16-21)

On another occasion, the Apostles were sitting in their boats dejected after spending all night fishing without a catch. This had gone on for a number of evenings and they were now desperate for a catch. It was then they noticed tongues of fire appeared above the rocks on the shore at the Sea of Galilee. There Jesus appeared and walked along the shore line calling out and instructing the apostles to cast their nets on the other side of the boat and the miracle of a huge collection of fish resulted. So much so that they could hardly haul in the catch.

In a symbolic way, the fishing vessel is representative of the church, and the apostles and the catch of fish represent the parallel of many souls who follow Christ being caught by the fishermen whom Christ had taught to be fishers of men.

Whilst there are many myths, symbols and signs to guide one in faith in the risen Christ, it is worth of consideration to reflect on some of these for our spiritual benefit. The obvious ones are the symbols of Christ crucified and the empty cross, symbolic of the Risen Christ on and after Easter Sunday celebrations. The four evangelists themselves have symbols representing their power and ability as authors of the Gospels of the New Testament told for our spiritual well-being. Matthew is sighted as the winged man, whilst Mark is a winged lion, and Luke a winged bull, with John soaring above as an eagle. They all are represented with wings, like angels of the heavens. Then the New Testament writings of the Apostles have Andrew as one in sandals with fish or a rope in hand, whilst Bartholomew is depicted bearing a knife in his hand.

Then comes James, known as 'the son of Thunder,' who was reported to preach in Spain, resulting in many symbols that surround his name. For it is The Way of the Camino de Santiago from medieval times to the present day that symbolic reminders of his mission of preaching ' Faith without works is dead," in the Santiago way. The symbol of the pilgrim's staff, scallop shell, key, sword, pilgrim's hat, and his mythical appearance on a white charger in a Christian battle against the Moors are just some of the well-known symbols to those on Pilgrimages.   Then there is James son of Aplhaeus, whose symbol is of a square rule, club or saw; Jude as sword, club or ship, and Peter who was granted the keys to the kingdom of heaven by Christ, he is often depicted with a giant key in hand, or in a boat fishing, or on an inverted cross, for reported he was crucified upside down in Rome stating; " I am not worthy to be crucified facing upright like my Master." He is sometimes depicted holding a book or scroll, with a bushy beard and unruly hair. Philip is sometimes seen as holding a basket of loaves of bread and a cross. Simon with two fishes, Thomas with an axe or spear, and then comes Judas, with thirty pieces of silver!

Whilst these symbols have their place as timely reflections of one's faith and the duties imposed upon us for our salvation, there is no better guidance to faith than the gospels as a reflection of Christian belief. For they are lively conversations of claims and counter-claims of temptation, of faith, of forgiveness, of the words of redemption and of the belief in the afterlife beyond this earthly realm. Jesus too was tempted in the desert, and we pick up the biblical story of Jesus' baptism in the River Jordan by John The Baptist. It was John who lived for a time in the desert living on wild berries and locusts, and where it was revealed to him of the coming of a Saviour; where the revelations of the future were told to him.

We may well ask why Jesus used his baptism as the launchpad into his public ministry. It was soon after that that he found himself alone in the desert wilderness. Barren, lonely and inhospitable, Jesus finds himself in a land that bears little resemblance to the giving waters of the River Jordan. Surely there are better ways He could have used those forty days. In our Western society success is closely connected with speed and efficiency. Our performance is determined by how much we can achieve in a given eight-hour day, and how many of us define our self-worth by our output. Yet we see Jesus, freshly baptised and teeming with potential, spending forty days removed from people. He came to serve. One can only think of the words that would be used to describe a colleague who chose to take 40 days 'off' immediately after accepting a new position.

These are pivotal days in Jesus' ministry. The Spirit leads him to the desert to prepare Himself, and to ensure He is truly ready for the mission. The wilderness is presented as a place of preparation, a place of discerning God's voice, and a place of learning to trust God's great plan. It is no coincidence that the prescribed things Jesus is tempted with seem, at face value, to be good things. It is not as though Lucifer is enticing Jesus to lie, steal or commit murder. It is quite the opposite, the devil tempts Jesus with bread, scripture, and the kingdoms of this world. Indeed, it takes a relationship with God and a desire to know His will to distinguish between right from wrong. By tempting Jesus with bread, Jesus must choose between what He immediately wants and what the Father desires for His time on the earth. By tempting Jesus with holy words for evil purposes, Jesus is made to consider how easily scripture can be used to assert superiority. By tempting Jesus with the kingdoms of the world, Jesus is urged to consider the lucrative nature of power and wealth.

We see in the passage how a relationship with God and a deep desire to do His will is essential to our discernment process. The key to overcoming our defects of character and fighting temptation is to know God. When Jesus was tempted he suffered. When he fasted His body entered a weakened state, and in this way, he experienced what it is to be human. God desires us to enter a relationship with Him, and by being at our most human we are able to engage even more deeply in that relationship, knowing that Jesus personally our suffering. Like Jesus, it is in our weakened state that we hear the voice of the Father, without the things of this world to distract us. As Ashleigh Donnelly said: "Temptation can be an opportunity for us to turn to God…a reminder to listen out for the still, small voice of God within our hearts."

So here we now turn to those Gospel reflections written by Matthew and John that tell of the events of Jesus' transfiguration. "Six days later, Jesus took with him Peter and James and his brother John and led them up a high mountain, by themselves. And he was transfigured before them, and his face shone like the sun, and his clothes became dazzling white. Suddenly there appeared to them Moses and Elijah, talking with him. Then Peter said to Jesus, "Lord, it is good for us to be here; if you wish, I will make three dwellings here, one for you, one for Moses, and one for Elijah." While he was still speaking, suddenly a bright cloud overshadowed them, and from the cloud, a voice said, "This is my Son, the Beloved; with him I am well pleased; listen to him!" When the disciples heard this, they fell to the ground and were overcome by fear. Jesus came and touched them, saying, "Get up and do not be afraid." And when they looked up, they saw no one except Jesus himself alone. As they were coming down the mountain, Jesus ordered them, "Tell no one about the vision until after the Son of Man has been raised from the dead." (Matthew 17:1-9) Transformation is something we may encounter at a time of great change in our lives. It happened to Saul on the road to Damascus, when he encountered the risen Lord and was blinded by the light, regained his sight and was transformed from a Roman soldier who persecuted the followers of Christ to the greatest of missionary disciples. When Mary says ' yes' to the angel Gabriel at the Annunciation, (Luke 1:26-38) she is transformed into the Mother of Jesus, our Lord.

CHAPTER 8.

GOSPEL REFLECTIONS

Transfigured means " to be transformed into something more beautiful or elevated"; " transform outwardly, usually for the better." In Matthew's Gospel, we are invited to transform ourselves into something even more beautiful. Just as Jesus shows his divine self to Peter, James and John, he asks us to transform into something even more beautiful too. Jesus fills his disciples with hope so that in time they too can share the Good News of the spirit of Jesus with all.

Pope Francis summarises the transfiguration ascent of Jesus on the mountaintop and the descent down the mountain with the disciples after the event. " From the event of the Transfiguration, I would like to take two significant elements that can be summed up in two words: Ascent and descent. We all need to go apart, to ascend the mountain in a space of silence, to find ourselves and better perceive the voice of the Lord. This we do in prayer. But we cannot stay there! Encounter with God in prayer inspires us anew to ' descend the mountain' and to return to the plain where we meet many brothers weighed down by fatigue, sickness, injustice, ignorance, and poverty both material and spiritual. To these brothers in difficulty we are called to bear the fruit of that experience with God, by sharing the grace we have received.

"He that hath an ear, let him hear what the Spirit saith unto the churches; To him that overcomes will I give to eat off the tree of life, which is in the midst of the paradise of God." (Revelation 2:7).

The transfiguration reminds us that Jesus is the source of our strength; any light that shines comes from His grace and love. Just like Peter, James and John, we are invited to live as witnesses to Jesus' unconditional love. Through prayer, with others, in union, We can work towards receiving and being in the light accepting the greatest gift of all, The Grace of God.

So let us look at the story told in John's Gospel of the Samaritan woman: "So Jesus came to a Samaritan city called Sachem, near the plot of ground that Jacob had given to his son Joseph. Jacob's Well was there, and Jesus, tired out from his journey, was sitting by the well. It was about noon. A Samaritan woman came to draw water, and Jesus said to her, "Give me a drink." (His disciples had gone to the city to buy food.) The Samaritan woman said to him, "How is it that you, a Jew, ask for a drink from me, a woman of Samaria?" (Jews do not share things in common with Samaritans). Jesus answered her, "If you knew the gift of God and who it is that is saying to you, 'Give me a drink,' you would have asked him, and he would have given you living water." The woman said to him, "Sir, you have no bucket, and the well is deep. Where do you get that living water? Are you greater than our ancestor Jacob, who gave us the well and with his sons and his flocks drank from it?" Jesus said to her, "Everyone who drinks this water will be thirsty again, but those who drink of the water that I will give them will never be thirsty. The water that I will give will become in them a spring of water gushing up to eternal life." The woman said to him, "Sir, give me this water, so that I may never be thirsty or have to keep coming here to draw water." Jesus said to her, "Go, call your husband, and come back." The woman answered him, "I have no husband." Jesus said to her, "You are right in saying, 'I have no husband,' for you have had five husbands, and the one you have now is not your husband. What you have said is true!" The woman said to him, "Sir, I see that you are a prophet. Our ancestors worshipped on this mountain, but you say that the place where people must worship is in Jerusalem." Jesus said to her, "Woman, believe me, the hour is coming when you will worship the Father neither on this mountain nor in Jerusalem. You worship what you do not know; we worship what we know, for salvation is from the Jews. But the hour is coming and is now here when the true worshipers will worship the Father in spirit and truth, for the Father seeks such as these to worship him. God is spirit, and those who worship him must worship in spirit and truth." The woman said to him, "I know that Messiah is coming" (who is called Christ). "When he comes, he will proclaim all things to us." Jesus said to her, "I am he, the one who is speaking to you."

Just then his disciples came. They were astonished that he was speaking with a woman, but no one said, "What do you want?" or, "Why are you speaking with her?" Then the woman left her water jar and went back to the city. She said to the people, "Come and see a man who told me everything I have ever done! He cannot be the Messiah, can he?" They left the city and were on their way to him.

Meanwhile, the disciples were urging him, "Rabbi, eat something." But he said to them, "I have food to eat that you do not know about." So the disciples said to one another, "Surely no one has brought him something to eat?" Jesus said to them, "My food is to do the will of him who sent me and to complete his work. Do you not say, 'Four months more, then comes the harvest'? But I tell you, look around you, and see how the fields are ripe for harvesting. The reaper is already receiving wages and is gathering fruit for eternal life, so that the sower and reaper may rejoice

together. For here the saying holds true, 'One sows and another reaps.' I sent you to reap that for which you did not labour. Others have laboured, and you have entered into their labour."
Many Samaritans from that city believed in him because of the woman's testimony, "He told me everything I have ever done." So when the Samaritans came to him, they asked him to stay with them, and he stayed there for two days. And many more believed because of his word. They said to the woman, "It is no longer because of what you said that we believe, for we have heard for ourselves, and we know that this is truly the Saviour of the world." (John 4:5-42).

This Gospel of John was no doubt written for a universal community living sixty years after Jesus' life, death and resurrection. The people have witnessed the destruction of Jerusalem and the temple; the apostles and disciples are all likely deceased; and Paul has taken the message of Jesus to the Gentiles of the Mediterranean. John uses dramatic imagery and metaphor to enable the reader, in this case us, to come to an encounter with Jesus- water collection, food gathering, community, personal and intimate relationships, travel, and religious practice are all experiences in daily life. They are also metaphors for the spiritual nourishment in our journey in friendship with Jesus.

In the living conversation of claim and counterclaim, we hear parts of the woman's life story in regard to her relationship failures, and her longing for the Messiah who will reveal the truth about all things. Jesus and the disciples stayed for two more days, and many became followers because of the testimony of the woman. "We no longer believe just because of what you said; now we have heard for ourselves, and we know that this man is really the Saviour of the world" (John 4:39-42). Before she even lays eyes on Jesus, this woman, in the deepest and most hidden part of her life, is desiring God in her life. There is an intimacy in this brief meeting that gives the woman a sense that the person of Jesus she encounters has always known her. His merciful love fills her with such joy she just wants to share it. She is bubbling over with it, she is transformed! As he walked along, he saw a man blind from birth. His disciples asked him, "Rabbi, who sinned, this man or his parents, that he was born blind?" Jesus answered, "Neither this man nor his parents sinned; he was born blind so that God's works might be revealed in him. We must work the works of him who sent me while it is day; night is coming when no one can work. As long as I am in the world, I am the light of the world." When he said this, he spat on the ground and made mud with the saliva and spread the mud on the man's eyes, saying to him, "Go, wash in the pool of Siloam" (which means Sent). Then he went and washed and came back able to see.

The neighbours and those who had seen him before as a beggar began to ask, "Is this not the man who used to sit and beg?" Some were saying, "It is he." Others were saying, "No, but it is someone like him." He kept saying, "I am the man." But they kept asking him, "Then how were your eyes opened?" He answered, "The man called Jesus made mud, spread it on my eyes, and said to me, 'Go to Siloam and wash.' Then I went and washed and received my sight." They said to him, "Where is he?" He said, "I do not know."

They brought to the Pharisees the man who had formerly been blind. Now it was a Sabbath day when Jesus made the mud and opened his eyes. Then the Pharisees also began to ask him how he had received his sight. He said to them, "He put mud on my eyes. Then I washed, and now I see." Some of the Pharisees said, "This man is not from God, for he does not observe the Sabbath." But others said, "How can a man who is a sinner perform such signs?" And they were divided. So they said again to the blind man, "What do you say about him? It was your eyes he opened." He said, "He is a prophet." The Jews did not believe that he had been blind and had received his sight until they called the parents of the man who had received his sight and asked them, "Is this your son, who you say was born blind? How does he now see?" His parents answered, "We know that this is our son and that he was born blind; but we do not know how it is that now he sees, nor do we know who opened his eyes. Ask him; he is of age. He will speak for himself." His parents said this because they were afraid of the Jews; for the Jews had already agreed that anyone who confessed Jesus to be the Messiah would be put out of the synagogue. Therefore his parents said, "He is of age; ask him." So for the second time, they called the man who had been blind, and they said to him, "Give glory to God!   We know that this man is a sinner." He answered, "I do not know whether he is a sinner. One thing I do know, though I was blind, now I see." They said to him, "What did he do to you? How did he open your eyes?" He answered them, "I have told you already, and you would not listen. Why do you want to hear it again? Do you also want to become his disciples?" Then they reviled him, saying, "You are his disciple, but we are disciples of Moses. We know that God has spoken to Moses, but as for this man, we do not know where he comes from." The man answered, "Here is an astonishing thing! You do not know where he comes from, and yet he opened my eyes.

We know that God does not listen to sinners, but he does listen to one who worships him and obeys his will. Never since the world began has it been heard that anyone opened the eyes of a person born blind. If this man were not from God, he could do nothing." They answered him, "You were born entirely in sins, and are you trying to teach us?" And they drove him out. Jesus heard that they had driven him out, and when he found him, he said, "Do you believe in the Son of Man?" He answered, "And who is he, sir? Tell me, so that I may believe in him." Jesus said to him, "You have seen him, and the one speaking with you is he." He said, "Lord, I believe." And he worshipped him. Jesus said, "I came into this world for judgment so that those who do not see may see, and those who do see may become blind." Some of the Pharisees near him heard this and said to him, "Surely we are not blind, are we?" Jesus said to them, "If you were blind, you would not have sin. But now that you say, 'We see,' your sin remains.

The pilgrim trudged on through the lonely night in search of his heart's desire. He could hardly see the track ahead because the sky was pitch black and his fading headlamp seemed to be the only brightness in his life. His mood was melancholy but his seeking led to inward consolation. Then he shouted aloud to the universe: "I will hear what the Lord God speaks within me," and he received comfort from these words. He had come to a place of recognition that he was now living in this world but was no longer of it. He suddenly found that he was walking with another who began to speak to him. Although He could not identify the shadowy figure that he walked near, he was soothed by the words he spoke to him: "Blessed are the ears that listen to the Truth teaching inwardly, for they are not of this world. Blessed are the eyes that are closed to outward things, but open to inward things, and daily prepare themselves to revive the secrets of heaven."

The shadow companion continued " Blessed are those who strive to devote themselves wholly to God, and free themselves from the entanglements of the world. Consider this fellow traveller, shut the door against the desires of the senses, so that you may hear what the Lord and your God speak within you."

The Pilgrim sensed that he was in the presence of The Lord, the 'Manifest One' whom he had but recently learnt to put his trust in, for he believed in the Risen Lord. " I am your salvation, your peace, and your Life, keep me close and you shall find peace. Set aside the things of time, and seek eternity; for what are the things of time but deceits; And how can any creature help you, if your Creator has abandoned you? Set aside, therefore, all else, and make yourself acceptable to your Creator, and be faithful to Him, that you may lay hold of true blessedness." The Pilgrim then replied:

"Speak on Lord, for your servant listens. For I am your servant; grant me understanding, that I may know Your testimonies." He paused for a breath before continuing: " The prophets preached and enlightened with your word, but they cannot bestow your spirit. The prophets speak most eloquently, but if you are silent, my heart's desire can not ignite. They instruct and you open up understanding. They set forth the mysteries, and you reveal the meanings of all secrets. They teach your commandments, but you helped us to observe them. They point the way, but you grant us strength to follow. When my action is external; You instruct and enlighten the heart. They water the seed; You make it fruitful. They proclaim the words, but You impart understanding to the mind. You have the words of eternal life, speak to me: Lord for your servant listens."

CHAPTER 9.

THE MANIFESTED ONE

Christ: "My son, hear my words. They are surpassing sweetness, and excel all the learning of the philosophers and wise men of the world. My words are spirit and life, not to be quoted in vain pleasure, but are to be heard in silence, and received with all humility and love.   Pilgrim: " Blessed is the man that you instruct and teach him out of the law. You refresh him on evil days, and he will not be desolate on the earth."

Christ: I have taught the prophets from the beginning of the world, and do not cease to speak to all men today; but many are hardened, and deaf to my voice. Many listen more willingly to the world following the desires of the body rather than what is pleasing to God. The world promises passing rewards of little worth, and is served with great eagerness; I promise eternal and rich rewards, yet the hearts of men are indifferent to them."

Christ pauses then continues: " Who is there who serves and obeys Me with as great devotion as he serves the world and its rulers?" Christ sighs: " For a small reward man will hurry away on a long journey, for eternal life many will hardly take a single step. Men seek petty gains; they will quarrel shamefully over a single coin; for a mere trifle or vague promise, they will toil day and night. Oh, it is a great shame!   For an imperishable good, for a reward beyond all reckoning, for higher honour and glory without end, they are unwilling to endure little toil."

"My son, many are often deceived in their vain hopes, but none are misguided in My promises, and I never sent away empty-handed to anyone who trusts in me. I am the reward in all good men. So my pilgrim friend write my words in your heart, and meditate on them earnestly; they will aid you in temptation. Whatever you do not understand when you read, you shall know in the days of My coming to you. I visit my chosen in two ways; with trial and consolation. Day by day, I teach them two lessons, one in which I correct their faults, and the other in which I encourage them to progress in virtue," ' He who hears My words and despises them as I will judge him on the Last Day.'

The curtain of darkness slowly dissipated as the morning twilight shone, opening up the vista of the valley floor below. The pilgrim made it to the top of the mountain as the sun appeared on the distant horizon. The exhilaration of the climb in that morning glow refreshed the pilgrims' spirit and he rested for a short while to drink some water before lifting up his backpack to continue the journey. The Albergue he had stayed in the previous night was crowded and he had difficulty sleeping; what with all the noise of snoring and farting from nearby fellow travellers and the flashing lights of Italian bike riders as they gathered their belongings and took to the road. It was around 3. a.m. and it was then the pilgrim got up and began his trudging up the mountain in the darkness. He was glad he had made the effort, for he may not have had the opportunity to speak to his Lord and listen to his guidance otherwise. Christ had given him a final instruction before he faded into the heavens: " My son, walk before Me in truth, and constantly seek Me in simplicity of heart."
The pilgrim's religious instruction of his youth he now recalled as he walked along the mountain track mindful of the little mountain village he was heading for breakfast as his tummy rumbled. What was it his religious instructor had taught about Christ's request? 'He who walks with me in truth shall be protected against the assaults of evil; truth shall deliver him from his defects and from the slanders of the wicked. Truth sets you free, you are really free, and need care nothing for the vain words of man.' He had to admit to

himself that his egocentricity and vanity of glory-seeking had formally led him down a path of rack and ruin for many a long day. He had climbed the ladder of success and achieved all the accolades that any man might wish for, but he had ruined his health in excesses of smoking, drinking, and all the seven deadly sins of pride, covertness, lust, anger, gluttony, envy and sloth. He had allowed his defects of character to take the upper hand in the pursuit of earthly goals, and the artificial nature of it all was now very apparent to him. The many 'slings and arrows of outrageous fortune' had come down upon him, and he had collapsed under the weight of it all. The ego self had deceived him into believing that he was all things to all people, like a grain of sand upon the beach of life that thought it was the beach. He knew now that the ego, whilst a necessity into action, had to be humbled and not puffed up into things contrary to his nature. He was learning about gratitude for the little things that came his way to soothe the savage beast within. He was aware of the fact that he could do nothing without God's grace, do nothing or have nothing without Him. For he alone could do all things, bestow all things, teach all things. He was learning to be as God dictates and found himself moving through each day without a plan.

The knowledge that he had accomplished many things of world value was no longer important to him. On this pilgrimage he was learning the lesson that Christ had been trying to get through to him for some time- teaching him to despise earthly things and love heavenly; to forsake this world, and to long for heaven. It was not that he needed to give up striving for necessities nor work to do creative things, but rather that with ego in check he could do these things for the benefit of others, and in turn be rewarded with the graces that only God could bestow. This indeed was his ultimate reward for the creative output that had been inflicted upon him. And he had a stark reminder as if by revelation, that he had a new-

found duty to love as he had never loved before. The Lord had foiled his mind with the thoughts that he had nothing of itself to boast about and many things of which to be ashamed, for he knew that he was much more wicked by his past actions than he had realised. He had chosen to repeat a mantra as he walked:
" Nothing I have done is of great importance. Let nothing seem great, precious or admirable capture my heart. Let nothing be high, praiseworthy or desirable, nothing worthy of regard, nothing high except that which is everlasting." He knew that if God so desired He would lead him by his creative efforts to do the things he had as natural talents in service of what God himself dictates. For this, the Pilgrim was born to, and despite difficulties, failures, and straying from the pathway of righteousness, he had always the opportunity in any given moment to start again in the service of his master, Christ the Lord- The One.

Then he became aware in a moment of awakening these words: "Stand in awe of God's judgment and fear the anger of the Almighty God. Do not presume to investigate the ways of the Most High, but rather examine yourself, see how greatly you have sinned through your defects of character not being kept in check, and see now how much good you can do by the lessons you have learnt through your trials and suffering, and by your lack of action in the things you have left undone."

And then more words poured forth from within him: " you have carried your devotion in books you have written, in the songs you have sung, in the visible signs of the way you have lived and the reputation you craved, but rarely have you served me with your heart and soul. There are those with enlightened minds and pure affection, who long for the kingdom of heaven. These I urge you to listen to for they are reluctant to be taken in by worldly matters, and many sacrifice themselves for the needs of their fellow man. I urge you to follow their example and not be taken in by the sins of the flesh, for Lucifer is ever present to tempt you to his way and not that of the Father. So be ever mindful and understand what the Spirit of Truth speaks within you and on the lips of the enlightened ones. For God teaches to despise earthly wisdom and to love the heavenly cause, forsaking all others to long for the eternal kingdom."

The pilgrim had tramped many kilometres over the hilltop and valley floor over the decades of his time in the wilderness. He had learnt to let go of the wounds of suffering he had endured in the past, learnt the wisdom of love over lust, been through the darkness into a new light and was learning to live, really live in the moment, and now he found he was on a different journey; an inward spiritual track into the unknown; a journey of enlightenment with God's guidance, not for earthly reward but for every word that he received from the mouth of God. The Manifest of Christ consciousness influenced him now more than ever before, as he trod the wilderness way of a newfound life.

A Prayer.

Deepen your love in me, O Lord, that I may learn in my inmost heart how sweet it is to love, to be dissolved, and to plunge myself into Your love. Let Your love possess and raise me above myself, with a fervour and wonder beyond imagination.
Let me sing the song of love. Let me follow You, my beloved, into the heights. Let my soul spend itself in Your praise, and rejoice for love. Let me love You more than myself, And myself only for Your sake. Let me love You for Your sake, Let me love all men who truly love You, as Your love commands, which shines out from You.

Let my soul find love in You alone; for You are the heart's true serenity, in You alone its sole abiding place, and outside Yourself all is hard and restless. This true peaceful place that is in You, the Sole, Supreme, and Eternal Good, I will dwell and take my rest. Amen"

And the pilgrim on the mountainside heard his innermost cry out to the heavens; "And how can I be aware of that love and what is it calling?" And a voice from the heavens answered him: "Love is swift, pure, tender, joyful, and pleasant. Love is strong, patient, faithful, prudent, long-suffering, vigorous, and never self-seeking. For when a man is self-seeking he abandons love. Love is watchful, humble, and upright; Love is not unpredictable and sentimental, nor is it intent on vanities. It is sober, pure, steadfast, quiet, and guarded in all the senses. Love is submissive and obedient to superiors, mean and contemptible in its own sight, devoted and thankful to God, trusting and hoping in Him even when not enjoying His sweetness; for none can live in love without suffering. Whoever is not prepared to endure everything, and to stand firmly by the will of the Beloved is not worthy to be called a lover. A lover must willingly accept hardship and bitterness for the sake of his Beloved, must never desert Him because of adversity." As the Pilgrim returned from his latest adventure, a journey of the Spirit for his betterment, he had learnt to his dismay how far he had drifted from the path of righteousness, the path that God had always had in his destiny. He knew that there would be other wandering adventures he would find himself on, but none would compare to the one he would ultimately turn to, for it was the way of his destiny that he was becoming more aware of, The way of Christ's consciousness, the way of the suffering soul that he must learn to endure. The pilgrim as a rover and wandering soul, lost in a former wilderness, had done his darnedest to abandon what he had begun, and any time trouble arose, he eagerly sought comfort in the things of the flesh. He was now in the realisation that a brave love, a warrior if you will, stands firm in temptation, and pays no heed to the craft arguments of Lucifer nor his dark angels. He is true to Christ of the Manifest, God in the reality of His infinite intelligence; For he knows now that Christ is He is true to the pilgrim in trouble as in prosperity. A wise lover values not so much the gift of love, as the love of the giver. He sees the affection above the gift and values every gift far below the Beloved. A noble love is not content with a gift but desires Christ above all gifts. All's not lost, therefore, if sometimes the pilgrim does not feel the devotion to Christ and the message of his saints that he desires to emulate. The pilgrim discerned that the good and pleasant affection which sometimes he enjoys is the effect of Christ's grace in him, and is a foretaste of the heavenly home of which he so ultimately yearns for within his soul. But he heard the warning that his analytical mind was telling him, not to rely on the joyous things too much, for it comes and goes. To fight against evil thoughts as they occur, and to reject with scorn the suggestions of the evil one, as a noteworthy sign of virtue and merit. Mindfulness of meditative practice had scorched his spirit with the remainder to let no strange fancies disturb from whatever source they may spring. Now that he had purpose he had to bravely hold on to it. He knew that the battle, like any soldier, may fall through weakness, but greater strength than before he could trust to draw on, for it is the abundant grace of God he could call upon at these times of trial. He knew he must guard against vain complacency and conceit, for by life experience, he knew it leads to too many errors, and causes almost incurable blindness of the heart. He knew that he had to overthrow his pride, which presumes its own strength; to be conscious of the warning and be of contrite heart and humility.

In the belief of spirituality, we are told by the wise of old that the earthly plane is a kind of school where human beings are invited to learn that they are spiritual beings with an inherited propensity for enlightenment as strong as the urge of seed to germinate as a plant, to break through the crap and crud, to seek the sun and flower to its true self. The world provides a learning space, a playground, wherein the seeker is guided through stages of an interior configuration of energy (Yastion, 2009).

CHAPTER 10.

THE SHADOW OF GOD

In a submission to Academia Letters, Marcelo Saad (2021) notes that the thing called " spirit " must exist. Saad points to the existence of abnormal phenomena like mediumship, memories of past lives, near-death, and end-of-life experiences to support this claim. Saad correctly notes that there is no materialist explanation for these phenomena and that therefore scientists should work towards developing a framework for theorising spirit. Saad points to Spiritism as a potential ground for theoretical exploration and the development of an " educated model of spirit and its nature."
Saad suggests the following Spiritism-inspired theoretical statements from which we might begin.
Spirit is an immaterial, eternal essence that is the root of human identity.
Spirit is beyond our knowledge and capacity.
Many of the characteristics and potentialities are blocked by matter.
The soul is the source of all mind properties manifested through the brain activity by awareness, thoughts, and emotions.
That the spirit exerts an incessant action upon all of us, sometimes promoting insight; however, some people can transmit a complete message (mediums).
That after death, the soul keeps its personality and knowledge from life experience.
That all spirits must pass through many incarnations for their learning and perfecting process; the new incarnation temporarily blocks access to past life data.

Whilst I agree with Saad's viewpoint that there is a need for science to incorporate the concept of spirit in an earnest attempt to explain by the study of human society belief and culture development phenomenon, for it might respond to the decades-old call to re-enchant and reinvigorate social behaviour, and physical science in a way that might help humanity evolve beyond the current political, economic, and ecological impasse; a stalemate which will certainly decimate human and animal populations if not resolved quickly.

One might well question the utility of Spiritism, or the traditional spirituality or religion for that matter, without being aware of the intersection of social- class, gender, and ethnicity. It is more apparent than ever that spiritual thought from the world viewpoint comes from a white supremacist, patriarchal, social class, and colonialist lens. And worst still, most spiritual systems are specifically modified or intentionally designed as tools of control, for suppression and oppression. I might continue along the pathway of an in-depth understanding view of the agenda of 21st-century science, political, social and beliefs it now stands and what needs to be done to change the un-emotional logical linear worldview on all things pertaining to the humanist control viewpoint to save the planet versus the spiritual viewpoint of love for fellow man and the actions necessary to ensure the heart of individuality gives of itself in consideration of others as Christ so dedicated to his teachings. The New Testament quotes Jesus as saying in Luke 18:25 "It is easier for a camel to pass through the eye of a needle than for a rich man to enter the kingdom of God." Further, Jesus said: "Truly I tell you, unless you change and become like little children, you will never enter the kingdom of heaven."

The paragraphs of this chapter lean a little too far away from what this book is about. It is easy to cast a critical eye over the world and take the 'God is dead' approach to deal with life, with all its troubles and strife and use the one world-order viewpoint of dealing with all of mankind, nature and change in the collective humanist approach of the elite, but it is not the answer for those of us who believe in the manifested One and in the infinite intelligence that in truth sorts order out of chaos and runs the show.
I can in my belief always deem faith in God, A Divine Being, an integral part of being human, be it secular or otherwise. As Ecclesiastic put it in the biblical quote: " God placed eternity in the hearts of every man," and whatever course society takes does not negate that. Whilst I'm opposed to the God of the Crusades, Colonialism, Auschwitz, and Apartheid, I don't believe a world without religion to be a Utopia; like John Lennon sang about in his hit song "Imagine."
" Where the fire of the religious imagination is extinct… there the existence of God becomes dead, a self-contradictory existence." (The Essence of Christianity, 1841 Ludwick Feuerbach). Secularisation brings along the death of God, which probably hides the death of the human being: the end of theology highlights the end of the study of human society, its culture and development. We as a worldview collective no longer believe, we only believe that we believe in the divinity and the humanity of the human being. We have 'retired' from having a strong religious or spiritual quality; indicating or suggesting the presence of the divinity. Therefore, to remain true to the One true God, to his Son, through his death, and resurrection, and to the third person of the Trinity, we have to learn to live and love in this world but not be of it. One has the choice of either being an enemy and annihilator of God or an ally of Him, a substance essence of the Trinity of Father, Son and Holy Spirit entity, who shares his creative traits and attributes. In

the latter case, the human being is an anointed " Mini- God", the authorised servant of a powerful master. In the former instance, the godless disbeliever desires something else entirely, perhaps a 'Superman' or a 'not-a- man, or perhaps he shall stand as an egocentric "God-man."

In 'The Ego and its Own' (1844) German philosopher Max Stirner had the thought: " At the entrance of modern times stands the ' God-Man'. At its exit will only the God in the God-man evaporate? And can the God-man really die if only the God in him dies? They did not think of this question, and thought they were finished when in our days they brought to the victorious end the work of Enlightenment, the vanquishing of God: they did not notice that man had killed God in order to become now - 'sole God on high'.God has had to give place, yet not to us, but to man. How can you believe that the God-man is dead before the man to him, besides the God is dead?" Man has killed God in order to become God- a satanic complex looking through the lenses of the rejection of religion and moral principles, in the belief that life is meaningless. Tio quotes the Latin: Deus est mortuus, ergo ego sum Deus- " God is dead, therefore I am God." But this is an unfinished part of the story for the God-man will only have died after the combined death of God and the human being. The ultimate aim of the Lucifer complex.

Les Chants de Maldoror (*The Songs of Maldoror*) is a French poetic novel written and published between 1868 and 1869 by the Comte de Lautréamont , the nom de plume of the Uruguayan-born French writer Isidore Lucien. The work concerns the antisocial character, a figure of evil who has renounced conventional morality. Although obscure at the time of its initial publication, *Maldoror* was rediscovered and championed by the Surrealist artists during the early twentieth century. The work's transgressive, violent, and absurd themes are shared in common with much of Surrealism's output. The gruesome killing of God echoes Jean-Paul Marat's comment: "And when I raised my eyes to the boundless world for the divine eye, it stared at me from an empty bottomless socket." In the sadistic nothingness of the Maldoror, he looks for God and finds not mankind's highest idea, but the personification of the negative nothing. The Artist Goya, in his depressive paintings on the walls of his hermitage, had many images. One of the theses, the painting of Saturn depicts a predator with a brain spilling blood over his beard that more precisely endorses the death of God and man: " I slowly raised my eyes, ringed with bluish circles, towards the concavity of the firmament and I, who was so young, dared to penetrate the mysteries of heaven! Not finding what I was seeking, I lifted my eyes higher, and higher still, until I saw a throne made of human excrement and gold, on which was sitting- with idiotic pride, his body draped in a shroud of unwashed hospital linen- he who calls himself the Creator! He was holding in his hand the rotten body of a dead man, carrying it in turn from his eyes to his nose and nose to mouth, and once it reached his mouth, one can guess what he did with it. First, he ate his head, then his legs and arms, and, last of all, the trunk, until there was nothing left; for he crunched the bones as well…And he would continue his savage meal, moving his lower jaw, which in turn moved his brain- blood splattered and a soaked beard. Oh! Reader, doesn't this last-mentioned detail make your mouth water?" Comte de Lautréamont (1869). It was no doubt Lautréamont's lament of formerly disguised piety signifying the horror of forever losing God. It is a hell to the deprivation of God's love that theologians tell us about, The deep circles of the inferno where hell loses reference to the idea of heaven, becoming hell unto itself. It must be argued for the majority of believers the question of the super-death of God is outrageous, because either they see divinity as an interventionist personal state of otherness, that provides meaning to their existence, or they are proud to inherit a somewhat mechanical faith from their ancestors, which gives them security in answers before all questions. Nevertheless, if the issues of the super death and the hell-in-itself can be theorised, even in a heretical vein, this means that a few individuals should struggle dramatically with these existential ideas, as systematic anomalies that refuse to take the easy way out and are unsatisfied with the common of common sense, putting freedom before happiness, having unanswerable questions. After all, the tremendous event is still on its way, wandering; it has not yet reached the ears of men," The shadow of God is everywhere, also in us, even if we are agnostics or atheists, because we are the products of two thousands years of religious programming. "And we- we must still defeat his shadow as well!" (Nietzche 1882, 1887).

Of what I say in the writings, theologies of the death of God and mankind, it is more relevant than ever in this 21st century. We must remember that the vision of those writings hails from the 19th century but applies to a greater depth today, for billions on this planet have already turned from God believing that life is all about living now and the God myth is dead, as they soon enough will be. So the view of "eat, drink and be merry for tomorrow we die" is the mantra of those who are already lost.

We know through medical science that the brain is divided into two parts, one side being the logical linear brain and the other the creative. In this world now everything is geared toward the logical linear aspects of living, and not so much the creative. For we are prone to act like the one-eyed giant of Greek mythology, stumbling, bumbling, and crashing through life without much thought of the consequence of our logical-liner half-brain existence. And now we have advanced (regressed ?) to artificial intelligence to do our thinking for us. In the mental madness of our existence, it is understandable that reason gives way to logic in the belief that we have to accept what is dedicated in a world of No-God concepts and that an ultimate No-man will be necessary, for robotology and algorithms is also taking over everything. Man, in his current state can easily fall prey to all the distractions that pleasure his senses that the world has to offer to the detriment of his immortal soul.

Let us not forget that man only uses ten per cent of his half-brain logical linear thought process, and that the other ninety per cent is an unknown void. It is that ten per cent that has concluded through study and non-belief indoctrination acceptance that God didn't make man but man-made God. A thinking brain can take a viewpoint of belief or non-belief in a Creator God just as easily as logic may discern. It is only one more step and No eternal life. However, man has another half brain and it is called the creative which has one hundred per cent capacity to use the creative imagination to believe and be guided by a creator God, in saving mankind, or the planets for example. More importantly, is the saving of one's own eternal soul and applying the marriage of the logical and the creative imagination and God becomes real, and our ever-present actions to his will that is the guiding light to our salvation in an afterlife is affirmed. How do I conclude this in my mind, heart and soul? Well, you may recall earlier in the book that I had gone to a great deal of research from ancient philosophers, written documentations of wise men of pre and post-Roman times, and those who scribed for the Caesars, and of course the Bible, to [prove to myself that The Lord Jesus Christ walked this earth.

This satisfied my logical linear half-brain belief, and the rest was an enlightenment of the creative brain, based on the death, resurrection and ascension of Christ into the heavens. So my creative imagination could now discern that there is a God of the manifest, The Risen Christ, who guides me and you into good orderly direction- right thinking. And he is the spiritual son of the most high; that infinite

intelligence that is the Almighty God. Then there's the spirit of the third person of this Trinity- The Holy Spirit that rains grace upon us as a consequence of the sacrifice that Christ made to forgive us for our defects of character, which the religions of our world call sin.
I was thinking of the pilgrim on his adventures who had the spiritual conversations of guidance with Christ that we spoke of earlier in this little work. Then the Spirit moved me from the beyond and I heard a former teacher in my head:" Grace is a Supernatural Gift imposed on us by God for our salvation" And it was then that the concealing Grace of God under humility came upon me. Then I heard, like that Pilgrim, the voice of Christ in the stillness of this hour: " My son, it is safer and better for you to conceal the grace of devotion; do not boast of it, do not speak much of it, and do not dwell much on it. It is better to think more humble to yourself and to fear that this grace has been granted to one who is unworthy of it. Never depend too much on those feelings, for they may rapidly change to the opposite.
When you enjoy such grace, consider how sad and needy you are without it. Progress in the spiritual life consists not so much in enjoying the grace of consolation, it is in bearing its withdrawal with humility, resignation and patience, neither growing weary in prayer and meditation nor neglecting other acts of devotion. Do willingly, and to the best of your ability and understanding, of whatever lies in your power, and do not neglect your spiritual life because of any dryness or anxiety of mind.
The voice of Christ faded into the void for a moment like the sound of His instruction was taken by the sound of the wind. I begin to think how remiss I am of regular prayer, meditation or humility and actions of a spiritual nature in most of my daily activities. The effect of hearing His voice, and the words he spoke left me speechless, but I resolved then to stop and take out my journal and write down the benefit of his meaning. I was thinking about something I heard many years before the wisdom of age set in: " The good die first and those

of us who remain travel through life in the main with hearts like dried-out sockets."

I was thinking back now to my former self. I had grown impatient when all didn't go according to my desire. I reasoned that life is not always in my control; it belongs to God alone to give and comfort when He wills, and whom He wills, just as he pleases and no more. I had formally focused on my goals and aspirations but lacked discretion, having brought ruin to those to whom I was entrusted. I was back then driven by power and control, a thirst to succeed come what may, and an unquenchable thirst for alcohol. I climbed to the top of the tree of the material world more than once only to find that the goal upon reaching my end goal was always empty. The money didn't fulfil my desire, the power that I wielded from my throne did little to benefit the masses I had been chosen to serve. My family benefited from the rewards I had accomplished but it was all about me, not them. I cared and was a provider but I did not love back then, as I had come to sadly realise.

In weighing up in my solitary genius starving for more of what the world has to offer, I had in my defects of character been rewarded with temporal success, ignorant of how small these things are in the face of God, for I had followed the prompting of my hearts desire rather than the dictates of reason. For I had presumed greater things than please God, and soon I lost all grace. I had overlooked the guidance of the teachers of my youth, who had aspired to teach me to build my nest in heavenly things.

Ultimately all that I had worked for disappeared- family, friends, business, and sadly some by their own hands had parted this world. My drinking increased as did my madness, for I had become a needy and wretched outcast, an uncontrollable alcoholic living like a hermit, desperate and alone. Women came and went throughout the years that followed. I had turned to women for comfort in the hope of overcoming my abandonment instead of turning to God. I didn't

realise it then but God was teaching me through humility and poverty of spirit, that I might learn to fly again with the wings of God instead of my former arrogance of flying by my own wings.
Eventually, I learnt to trust in the slow work of God, for the Greater Power allowed me the insight into a lotus flower of creative ideas, and through his guidance, I floated my boat of personality upon the living spiritual waters, trimmed my sail and flowed with the current. Initially, I had deceived myself, being still new to the spiritual adventure, but I had ceased drinking alcohol and was drawn then to wise counsel through the doors of Alcoholics Anonymous. Therein I learnt to 'let God and Let God' do his job for me. My life then was no longer about me but about God's guidance for me. It took a long time for me to follow the fellowships of AA's proven experience, to stay sober a day at a time rather than my own notions of what this newfound life is all about. I had to remind myself that those who are wise in their own conceit seldom humbly accept guidance from others. I had come to realise that a little knowledge and understanding tempered by humility is better than a store of learning coupled with vain complacency.

CHAPTER 12.

EPILOGUE.

God has granted me many talents, but it is better to have few talents than yield to conceit. I was (am) sober through the healing power of God and the programme of AA. I had to temper my elation and not forget my former spiritual poverty and fall from grace. For forgetfulness of the pure reverence of God is to lose the graces already given. God had taken away the despair and all my former troubles and adversity and was (is) teaching me to put my trust in him only. The Lord himself is reminding me that the man who feels secure in times of peace will often be discouraged and afraid in times of war. The course to remaining calm, cool and collected is to be careful to remain humble and modest in one's self esteem, and to direct and control the mind in meditative prayer, so that one may not return to falling into danger and disgrace. The spirit of devotion that God grants and the application of the Steps of Alcoholics Anonymous is aflame in the heart, but one must with a now sober mind consider how I will fare when the light leaves me. Sometimes God puts obstacles in our way and then the light of his guidance and that of the programme I am now devoted to act upon fades into darkness. I must remember when this happens, that the light will return in God's time. It is a warning to me for my own glory to enter further into the programme of AA, by helping others still suffering and the promised therein, by practicing the Steps of recovery.

I hasten to recall the wisdom of The One to whom this little book is devoted: " Trails are often more profitable than if all went in agreeable with you and in accordance with your wishes. For a man's merit is not to be reckoned by visions and comforts he may enjoy, nor by learning in the Scriptures, nor by being raised to high dignity. Rather it is by his grounding in humility and being filled with divine love;

by his pure constant and sincere seeking of God's glory; by his low esteem and honest depreciation of himself; and by his preference for humiliation and despite rather than honours at the hands of men.

Oh! I fear now in that humility, in the self-seeking and the glorious applause of men I still have a long way to go. For I still serve with my lips and the guidance of my pen and am often deceived by the Spirit that lives within linked to my defects of character; rather than the Holy Spirit of which you send to guide me. I wish to live for you alone but like St. Paul in his trials stated " For I do not understand my own actions [I am baffled and bewildered by them]. I do not practice what I want *to do,* but I am doing the very thing I hate [and yielding to my human nature, my worldliness—my sinful capacity]. (Romans 7:15). Paul of course continued in the service of the Lord despite his defects, for he managed to overlook his defects of character in preference to making Jesus his total mission. He went on to write and teach others to teach of the life of Christ and Christianity as we know has flourished to this very day as a consequence of his preaching zeal.

Likewise, a young Augustine was to write in his book of Confessions a most interesting reading. He was the young man who prayed "Lord, make me chaste (sexually pure) – but not yet!" He became a great intellectual, a professor of rhetoric in the city of Milan. He lived in relative luxury and enjoyed a life of sin. Augustine (354-430 C.E.), originally named Aurelius Augustine, became the Catholic bishop of Hippo in northern Africa. He was a skilled Roman-trained rhetorician, a prolific writer (who produced more than 110 works over a 30-year period), and by wide acclamation, the first Christian philosopher. It was Augustine who acclaimed; " do with me as you will, for I am in your hands; guide me according to Your will. I am indeed your servant and am ready for anything. I wish to live, not for myself but for You alone; how I wish I could serve You perfectly and worthily!"

Augustine continued: "Your grace, O pray; let it dwell in me, work in me, and abide in me to the end. Grant me always to will and desire whatever is most pleasing and acceptable to You. Let Your will be mine, and let my will ever follow and be confirmed wholly to your own. Let me be unable to ever will otherwise then your will, or do not will. Grant that I may die to all in this world, and for Your sake, love to be despised and unknown. Grant me above all else, to rest in You, that my heart may find peace in You alone; for You are the heart's true peace, its sole abiding place, and outside Yourself all is hard and restless. In this true serenity and peace that is in You, the sole, supreme, and eternal Good, I will dwell and take my rest. Amen. "

My route in this modern world, if I am to take the Manifested One as my rule and guide, is to use as my template the Steps of Alcoholics Anonymous in the sure and pleasant hope that I do God's will and that the promise assured by this programme of sobriety and spiritual progress may come to light in the sure belief that God is doing for me what I cannot do for myself.

So it is that this little work has come to an end and I leave you dear reader with the Steps and Promise of Alcoholics Anonymous that they may bring you solace and guidance as I trust this little work herein may do too.

AA's 12 Steps are based on the premise that turning one's life over to a personal "Higher Power," is the key to recovery.

Step 1: Admit your life has become unmanageable powerless over alcohol, people places and things.
Step 2: Accept that you need God to become sober 'Come to believe in a power greater than self.'
Step 3: Decide to turn over your will and life to the care of God as we understand him.
Step 4: Honestly take stock of your life by writing down a personal inventory of those you have harmed.
Step 5: Admit you're wrong to yourself, God, and others the exact nature of your wrongs.
Step 6: Be ready to have God remove your character defects by taking action to right the wrongs.
Step 7: Ask God to remove your shortcomings. **Pray for God to remove these defects and shortcomings so you can change your life for the better.**
Step 8: Write down everyone you've harmed during your addictions _ be willing to make amends to them all.
Step 9: Make amends to those you've harmed by being mindful that you don't cause additional pain as a consequence.
Step 10: Continue to honestly look at your actions and admit when you're wrong.
Step 11: Pray to God for direction and the power to follow those directions. Thought through prayer and meditation to do God's will in all things.
Step 12: Having had a spiritual awakening as a result of these steps we put into practice what you've learned and carry the message of faith and recovery to other addicts. The final step is to continue to practice the 12 steps throughout the rest of your life.

The AA Promises.

1. Our whole attitude and outlook on life will change.

2. Fear of people and of economic insecurity will leave us.

3. We will intuitively know how to handle situations that used to baffle us.

4. We will suddenly realise that God is doing for us what we could not do for ourselves.

5. If we are painstaking about this phase of our development, we will be amazed before we are halfway through.

6. We are going to know a new freedom and a new happiness.

7. We will not regret the past nor wish to shut the door on it.

8. We will comprehend the word serenity and we will know peace.

9. No matter how far down the scale we have gone, we will see how our experience can benefit others.

10. That feeling of uselessness and self-pity will disappear.

11. We will lose interest in selfish things and gain interest in our fellows.

12. Self-seeking will slip away.

AA Serenity Prayer.

"God, grant me the serenity to accept the things I cannot change, the courage to change the things I can, and the wisdom to know the difference."

Meditation For The Day

The grace of God cures disharmony and disorder in human relationships. Directly you put your affairs, with their confusion and their difficulties, into God's hands. He begins to effect a cure of all the disharmony and disorder. You can believe that He will cause you no more pain in the doing of it than a physician who knows how to effect a cure would cause a patient. You can have faith that God will do all that is necessary as painlessly as possible. But you must be willing to submit to His treatment, even if you cannot now see the meaning or purpose of it.

Prayer For The Day

I pray that I may willingly submit to whatever spiritual discipline is necessary. I pray that I may accept whatever it takes to live a better life.

About The Author.

Doug McPhillips, poet, singer, songwriter, and author commenced his journey of discovery over a decade ago as a result of life-changing experiences.

The many tracks he has traversed in Spain, Ireland, New Zealand and Australia have resulted in novels of myth, legends, folklore and self-evaluation for the enjoyment of his readers.

Doug sings and has recorded many of the songs that came to him on his travels. He sings with a majestic melody in true Australian style. Doug has written books on his Camino journeys, One World Government, poetry, biographies and an autobiography.

Doug is an adventurer who divides his time between creative pursuits, love for family and friends, and those who may benefit most from his efforts and experience.

Worldwide Publishers.
IngramSpark
1 La Verge TN37086
Nashville, Tennessee.

Printed in Australia
Lightning Source
76 Discovery Road South
Scoresby, Victoria 3179

www.ingramcontent.com/pod-product-compliance
Lightning Source LLC
Chambersburg PA
CBHW060522010526
44107CB00060B/2655